In the City of
Neighborhoods

In the City of Neighborhoods

◆

Seattle's History of Community Activism and Non-Profit Survival Guide

Arthur J. O'Donnell

iUniverse, Inc.
New York Lincoln Shanghai

In the City of Neighborhoods
Seattle's History of Community Activism and Non-Profit Survival Guide

iUniverse, Inc.

For information address:
iUniverse, Inc.
2021 Pine Lake Road, Suite 100
Lincoln, NE 68512
www.iuniverse.com

ISBN: 0-595-33792-9

Printed in the United States of America

Contents

Section Two: It's My Backyard, Too

Introduction: In the City of Neighborhoods

FOR A PERIOD OF AT LEAST 15 YEARS, from about 1965 through 1980, the United States witnessed a tremendous surge in political and economic activism at the community level. The efforts of neighborhood-based councils and the social services offered by not-for-profit organizations formed what was recognized as a national "neighborhood movement."

These activities came about in response to the actions of government. On one hand, governmental policies and agencies encouraged and paid for community organizing efforts. On the other hand, government sponsored highway projects, urban redevelopment programs, and other bureaucratic decisions gave neighbors plenty of reasons to join together in protest. Protests, however, are not the only measure of community activism.

"In the City of Neighborhoods" was a twenty-one part series of radio programs exploring the history and directions of the neighborhood movement in one particularly active community, Seattle, Washington. During the period in question, the city earned a national reputation as a place where citizens take an active role in governmental decision making and in finding solutions to the problems of urban life.

Seattle, of course, was not alone. Other cities—from Portland, Maine, to Kansas City, Missouri, and from Milwaukee, Wisconsin, to San Diego, California—engender a sense of neighborhood identity among citizens and mirror many of the types of programs and activities that are documented in this series. And while this project is locked into a specific time and place, many of the themes described herein can be found at work today (and will be in the future) in many American communities.

Far from being an epitaph for a dying movement, "In the City of Neighborhoods" is a testament that community activity of the 1970s was in reality another stage in the broader social movement that stretched through the 20th century. With its roots in the labor movement and community organizing of the early decades of the century, the social clubs of the 1920s, the Civil Rights movement of the 1940s through the 1960s, and the peace protests of the Viet Nam era, the neighborhood movement provided another stepping stone for activism, and another facet in the framework of social changes that continue to this day.

The two major sections of the project deal with the activities of Seattle-area community councils and neighborhood groups, and the work of non-profit social service organizations. While there are a plethora of community groups, these two major categories can be seen as the most active elements of the neighborhood movement of the 1970s and those most affected by changes in government priorities—at all levels—in the early 1980s.

The Neighborhood Movement

During the 1970s, neighborhood groups and community organizations rose to prominence and generated great amounts of media attention by addressing the social and political issues of urban living. Activity at the local level became so widespread that observers declared it to be a part of a "neighborhood movement."

"One clearinghouse of information about neighborhood activism in New York City found that since the mid-1970s several thousand block clubs had formed, addressing issues ranging from rent- and crime-control to healthcare and urban gardening. The National Commission on Neighborhoods compiled a list of over eight thousand larger community groups in the nation. In a *Christian Science Monitor* poll of communities with populations over 50,000, one third of residents claimed to have already taken part in some kind of neighborhood protest or improvement effort, and a majority declared their willingness to take some sort of direct action in defense of their neighborhoods in the future" (Morris & Hess, *Neighborhood Power*, Beach Press, 1975).

In all, some 20 million persons were estimated to be active members of community-based organizations during the 1970s, according to Harry Boyte, author of *The Backyard Revolution* (Temple Press, 1980).

Because it lacked an overt affiliation with left-wing, anti-war politics of the 1960s, the community movement was dismissed and ridiculed by some members of the traditional left. It was felt that the concern with family, property rights and other home-centered issues in the neighborhoods was actually a trend towards conservatism on the part of participants.

In reality, the ideals of the community movement shared much with progressive social activism dating back more than 50 years, and especially akin to 60's-style attempts to win greater degrees of decision-making power in a governmental system that was seen as huge and dehumanized in its efforts to resolve social issues. One *Christian Science Monitor* report called these efforts, "a groundswell movement of citizens calling for return of political and economic power to the local level."

The movement shared a common legacy with the Progressive Era and the Labor Movement of distant decades, noted Boyte. "Despite their differences, all have themes in common that roughly define the 'citizen advocacy' tradition. They represent an old American practice of co-operative group action by ordinary citizens motivated both by civic idealism and by specific grievances."

Commentators have indicated two distinct spheres of influence sought by citizen activists. One is the creation of permanent political structures that attend to issues of control and governance; the other involves representatives of the poor and special constituencies who seek to secure and deliver social services. Within these two spheres are included many different kinds of groups and organizations.

Here's an incomplete listing of types of groups that were active on the Seattle scene, according to city planner Steve Shepherd: "social clubs, fraternities and ethnic clubs, geographic-specific neighborhood organizations, government-sponsored Community Action Programs, umbrella organizations, which combine those various groups, non-profit social service organizations and single-issue coalition groups."

What is a Neighborhood?

The idea of community is a much-debated concept among academic observers and activists themselves. At its simplest, community can be defined as a "tie that binds" individuals into groups with recognizable common interests. These ties can include religion, ethnicity, land, corporate charter, civic organization, market place, collective enterprise and civil morality (like the Temperance Movement).

Perhaps the most easily identifiable constituents of the neighborhood movement are those that represent (or purport to represent) geographic neighborhoods. In Seattle, for instance, there are 113 neighborhoods recognized by city planners. Most of these neighborhoods have identifiable boundaries and characteristics, and at least one organization that claimed to represent the interests of local residents. If physical boundaries are not obvious, some neighborhoods are best defined by proximity to landmarks, schools or churches—say, the University District. In other cities, church parishes might form the most readily recognized neighborhood boundaries.

Most of Seattle's neighborhoods were formally delineated in a school district study conducted in the early 1960s.

Neighborhoods obviously provide a binding tie of locality for their residents, and community organizers fully exploit such ties. Neighbors share amenities as well as problems. All neighbors of a block can claim a nearby park as a resource; each may count an eyesore building or the presence of rats as a shared problem.

Community organizers became skilled in using this shared sense to bring people together. Examples given by activists include "crime watch" programs and clean-up days at local parks, gardens or other publicly owned lands. All such efforts are made easier because of the common tie of neighborhood proximity.

Community organizing can also build on fundamental institutions rather than geography. Groups that follow the precepts of organizer Saul Alinsky rely heavily on churches as a base for organizing people. Often, church groups will combine with neighborhood groups to address social needs. For instance, when neighbors in Seattle's Wallingford neighborhood decided to organize a block-watch system to combat increased crime, the program found a headquarters at the local United Methodist Church but was led by the president of the local community council.

Churches represent stable, on-going organizations whose members often share the common bonds of religion, culture and locality, while also expressing a deep concern for human needs. No wonder churches played such a significant role in the neighborhood movement.

The Federal Government and Communities

Community groups often gain political legitimacy and economic support from their greatest single adversary—the federal government.

The move towards encouraging citizen participation was incorporated in federal laws in numerous ways, many of which eventually backfired on bureaucrats who found themselves confronted with lengthy battles over policies and projects. Prominent examples include Urban Renewal and development of the interstate highway system.

Billed as a slum-clearance program to set the stage for improved housing opportunities for low-income families, Urban Renewal aggravated the housing problem by demolishing more low-cost homes than were ever built in replacement, displacing nearly 300,000 families and 150,000 other individuals.

Federal highway projects raised the ire of communities across the nation. At one point in 1970, nearly 400 communities were involved in disputes over highway construction projects and the urban dislocation they caused.

At the very same time, other federal programs were mandating citizen participation, teaching the techniques of organization, and providing a basis for communities to influence decisions about the distribution of federal funds.

One of the most important of these programs was the Model Cities Program legislated in 1966. Model Cities attempted an integrated approach to solving the problems of urban deterioration in housing, education, healthcare, transportation and recreation. Over 150 cities around the country shared $1 billion in aid.

In Seattle, as in other cities, the lasting legacy of Model Cities was less in forging permanent solutions to such problems than in getting citizens involved in the political process. Wording of the Model Cities Act mandated "maximum feasible participation" by affected communities.

While this phrase caused no end of problems for many interpreters, it seems to have been taken to heart in Seattle. The former director of the local Model Cities program and later the city's superintendent of parks, Walter Hundley, stated, "I don't think we would have had the strong neighborhood club, council movement in Seattle without Model Cities setting the pace."

Of course, Model Cities was not the only federal program with an impact on neighborhoods and community organizations. The 1960s and '70s saw a great deal of government resources directed to urban problems through categorical grants-in-aid. By 1980, $88 billion in directed grants were being administered under the federal budget.

When Richard Nixon became President of the United States, his administration altered the structure and the course of these types of grants.

Declaring a "New Federalism", Nixon instituted a revenue-sharing approach in which federal funds were funneled through state and local governments without many of the program requirements that characterized the grant-in-aid programs. A new development was the "block grant." While categorical grants were directed to specific purposes, block grants applied to broad functional categories, such as health and crime control.

Block grants became an important tool for community organizers following the implementation of Title I of the Housing and Community Development Act of 1974. Block grant funds were directed to cities, which often included community-based organizations in the spending decisions. CBOs and other groups became adept at vying for a piece of this federally funded pie.

Local Governments and Communities

According to Seattle city planner Steve Shepherd, neighborhood-based groups achieved legitimacy in their communities and at City Hall because of the availability of government money. Seen in another way, the expansion of government benefits through jobs, social services and project funding, gave a great motivation for community activists to pick fights with municipal agencies. A well-organized community group might win large concessions from politicians and bureaucrats to co-opt discontent.

Generally, the resources allocated to communities had their origins in the federal budget. But in Seattle, neighborhoods had an early experience with locally raised funding—money from the Forward Thrust bond issue of 1968.

At that time, voters in Seattle and King County approved a massive $120 million bond proposal for park acquisition and capital improvements for public facilities. Through the lobbying efforts of 22 existing community groups, $10 million in bond proceeds was set aside for use in neighborhoods, with priorities for spending to be determined by local residents. In addition, any capital improvements in neighborhoods had to conform to a resident-approved Neighborhood Improvement Plan.

This set the stage for a great flurry of neighborhood organizing in Seattle. Neighborhoods that already had community councils began work on neighborhood plans. Those that did not have formal representation became the focus of organizing efforts of a newly established Office of Neighborhood Planning.

Once again, the great irony of the neighborhood movement became apparent. On one hand, a city agency was helping neighbors join together to secure certain resources or to find help in solving local problems. On the other hand, activists would turn around and use these newly acquired resources and skills in fighting the policies of other city departments, such as engineering, parks, or even police.

A typical example comes when a neighborhood that had been organized through the efforts of the Neighborhood Planning office, would fight against the placement of low-income housing or a police precinct within its limits.

A Change in Government Policies

At the time this project was being put together, it was clear that a demonstrable change had occurred in the ways that government entities dealt with communities. Much of the change stemmed from the New Federalism policies begun by President Richard Nixon and resurrected by Ronald Reagan.

Through revenue sharing and block grants, the federal government had increased its ties with city governments and community groups—often bypassing states or even county-level governments. Categorical aid programs directed funding straight to non-profit social service agencies without another governmental intermediary.

But this situation changed dramatically, with the federal budget-cutting trend of the 1980s having a drastic impact on communities. One striking example was the impact on Community Action Programs (CAPs). In Seattle, the oldest and most established of these was the Central Area Motivation Program (CAMP).

Through the 1970s, CAMP received much of its funding though the Community Services Administration. CSA began its life as the Great Society's Office of Economic Opportunity, and was the home to many popular urban-oriented programs, including Head Start, VISTA, Legal Services and Upward Bound.

As part of the New Federalism budget cuts espoused by President Reagan, CSA was closed in October 1981. Its final budget of $525 million in 1981 had been used to fund over 1,600 local agencies and community development corporations that provided services for the poor. For fiscal year 1982, $360 million in former CSA money was converted into a new program, Community Service Block Grants, to be administered by states.

CAMP was one of 28 Community Action Programs in Washington State that went from receiving direct federal grants to competing for state allocations that were scheduled to halve each year. The effect on CAMP was quick and severe. In 1981, it had received $440,000 directly from CSA. Under the block grant format, this allocation was cut to $275,000 and in the next year reached $81,000.

Another example of the effects of New Federalism policies can be seen in the transition of Seattle's Public Health Hospital from a federal facility to a municipal corporation. The change came about in response to federal plans to close down the public-health hospital system, first enunciated in the 1970s but carried out by Reagan appointees.

These hospitals had a history nearly as old as the Republic, having served veterans and merchant seamen—in effect, they were the nation's first veterans' hospitals. By the 1970s, only eight such facilities remained, and the federal government decided they had outlived their usefulness. What was discovered in Seattle and other places was that the hospitals had been adapting to changing needs by including more community services and care for low-income citizens.

For instance, the Seattle Public Health Hospital had begun a unique relationship providing secondary care for neighborhood clinics throughout the city.

Fearing the loss of this valuable service backstop, a group of business, community and government leaders joined repeatedly to fend off closure efforts during the Nixon, Ford and Carter administrations. However, when Reagan took office, the end of the line was drawn. The community had to take control over the facility. With a great deal of political maneuvering, this was accomplished in autumn 1981. At the time, Seattle and Baltimore were the only two cities able to transfer their Public Health Hospitals to community corporations.

There are many other ways that the change in governmental policies affected communities, but the biggest impact was a shift of monetary resources away from community concerns and a transfer of decision making away from localities. Neighborhood groups found themselves competing for ever-shrinking shares of federal dollars.

Non-Profit Survival

In the battle over the 1982 federal budget, it became clear that not-for-profit organizations would be hurt even more than community activism. Military spending became a higher priority than healthcare and while media and politicians used the words "budget cuts" the action really amounted to a budget transfer. More than $40 billion in social service cuts ended up in the Pentagon budget.

Because of the president's stated desire to reduce government bureaucracy, federal and state employees became the largest category of newly unemployed in 1982. This meant that many services formerly provided by government agencies would either be taken up by other entities or they would disappear.

With "voluntarism" being promoted by the Reagan administration, the job of picking up the pieces fell to the non-profit sector. According to the group Independent Sector, in the early 1980s nearly one in seven dollars of the Gross National Product flowed through the non-profit sector. That does not even count volunteer efforts, cooperatives, self-help projects or other activities that are difficult to monetize. Independent Sector estimated that 84 million Americans regularly volunteered time to community projects. If a dollar amount were applied to that activity, it would be on the order of $65 billion annually.

Because of cutbacks in government services, non-profit groups simultaneously faced both an increasing load of responsibility and a loss of funding. A shakeout of organizations meant that many would close their doors while all others would need to closely examine and modify their organizations and services to adapt.

Groups previously reliant on government funding sources turned increasingly to corporations and private foundations for support. But reliance on the public sector proved to be risky and it would have taken a huge increase in private support to make up for the loss of federal dollars. Even corporate leaders who were very active in philanthropic programs agreed that, dollar for dollar, there was no way that the private sector could fully compensate for federal cuts.

But there was a decided upsurge in giving. Corporate contributions increased from $2.5 billion in 1980 to $3 billion in 1981, while the level of foundation giving held steadily at $2.5 billion. The recorded increases in private funding in 1981 amounted to about 25 percent of the federal cuts, and a far smaller percentage of state and local budget cuts.

One Seattle example of a program to deal with this situation was called Project Transition, sponsored by the King County United Way. This short-term project was established to identify and give aid to non-profit groups that provided services in the categories most affected by the federal cutbacks. About $1.5 million was raised from local corporations to be directed to emergency food and shelter programs, chore services for the elderly, daycare for welfare mothers, and to health clinics.

The intent of Project Transition was not merely to shift dependency from the government to corporate funding. It was meant to buy time, to give emergency service groups more of an opportunity to adjust.

Thinking Like a Business

Faced with such tectonic shifts in their funding prospects, many non-profits tried to develop a more businesslike approach to their missions. The 1980s were all about government shedding tasks best left to the competitive marketplace, and many professed the need to become more entrepreneurial and businesslike.

In a competitive market, they said, the prize goes to those groups with the most corporate-like image and the best information, and to those most savvy in adjusting to dynamic situations. In other words, groups needed to become entrepreneurs to survive and create new funding opportunities.

In a system of private patronage, it would be the entrepreneurs who gain the attention and assistance of corporations. Such a system would stress efficiency in administration, budget restraints, and reliance upon proven models of success. As former Treasury Secretary William Simon once stated: "Every corporation should spend every dollar of every contribution with the same care and attention it spends on employee pay and new plant and equipment. Decisions about corporate contributions should also be made on the same level as corporate investments. In effect, we should apply zero-based budgeting to institutions. Because we gave to them last year, let's ask whether money given to that cause is still serving its original purpose, or whether it could better serve that purpose someplace else."

Such an extreme creed did not become the rule of the 1980s, but community groups that appealed to such thinking were better able to win corporate contributions in a highly competitive environment.

Two perfect examples would be the Neighborhood Reinvestment Corporation's housing rehabilitation programs and The Nature Conservancy's land trusts. Each group attained a continued level of successful operations because they adopted businesslike methods. In other words, they called themselves "investments" instead of donations.

Advisors to non-profit groups counseled their clients to think beyond reliance on contributions. They offered seminars to promote ideas for starting businesslike enterprises to generate revenues. Skills workshops taught staff and volunteer board members the ins-and-outs of management while keeping on the Internal Revenue Service's good side.

This segment of "City of Neighborhoods" highlighted several types of entrepreneurial activities pursued by Seattle-area groups. The first way to improve revenues is to begin charging for some services, at least in ways compatible with the spending ability of clients. Frequently, this means using a sliding scale of prices based on income levels. For example, a community clinic would offer its low-income clients lower prices on routine medical and dental services.

Trends in revenue generating approaches often directly related to the organization's mission. The Randolph Carter Industrial Workshop, for instance, set up six satellite work programs to create jobs for its clients. These included janitorial and landscaping services, low-technology manufacturing, and a catering service. The programs not only provided revenue but offered valuable job skills. The Workshop boasted near self-sufficiency in the early 1980s.

Arms-length business developments might take the form of establishing investment trusts for endowments to diversify revenue sources. Another trend of the time was an emphasis on improvements to fiscal management, operations and processes. In this regard, the coincidence of computer technologies and access also meant increased spending for modern systems.

In Seattle, one solution took the form of consortiums or umbrella organizations that jointly managed operations and purchasing for several groups. The radio series highlighted three healthcare consortia, the oldest of which—Neighborhood Health Centers—had already existed for 10 years.

Conclusion

The community movement of the 1970s underwent a transformation in response to economics and political realities. Neighborhood groups and non-profit organizations alike found that standard practices were challenged. To continue being relevant to their constituencies, the groups were forced to re-examine their roles, create a new basis of economic stability and assess the needs of a new decade. Many survived, many didn't.

Section One: In the City of Neighborhoods

Part I: The Neighborhoods

Dedication, Voices of Seattle   3:40
The introduction to the series and homage to community activity in Seattle. Features the voices of citizens who participated in community activities, as recorded by the Neighborhood News Review project, 1979–81.

The Death of the Neighborhood Movement?   4:30
While some skeptics contended the neighborhood movement could not survive changes in government policies and support, the underlying concerns of communities remain. The rise of broader issues is seen as the next step for the community movement to take.

How Many Communities?   5:04
Presents various types of community organizations that played a role in the neighborhood movement, with comments from representatives of social clubs, community councils, umbrella groups, community action programs, non-profit service groups and single-issue advocates.

What is a Neighborhood?   4:48
The ways that neighbors perceive their communities and affinities, and how they get together for action.

Roots of the Neighborhood Movement   5:28
Development issues in Seattle and government programs spurred community organizing in the 1960s and 1970s: Model Cities, Forward Thrust and the fight against the R.H. Thompson Expressway.

Tactics of Community Organizing   4:12
Groups can decide to cooperate with or confront government agencies. This looks at how some groups achieved their goals.

CAMP—The Central Area Motivation Program   5:00

CAMP was typical of certain kinds of community groups that benefited from federal support of the Great Society. In the Reagan '80s, CAMP is among those hardest hit by budget cuts.

The City and the Neighborhoods   4:55

The City of Seattle specifically aided development of community organizations. Changes in municipal priorities are stealing resources and attention away from the neighborhoods.

The New Federalism and Block Grants   4:57

Budget cutbacks and transfers of federal programs to the states were all part of Reagan administration's policies affecting communities.

Public Health Hospital   5:10

Seattle showed its ability to adapt to changing tides of politics and economics when it won community control over this historic federal hospital.

The Home of the Good Shepherd   5:40

This former Catholic school and home for wayward girls is now home to many community organizations and arts groups in Seattle's Wallingford neighborhood.

Part II: Non-Profit Survival Guide

Thinking Like a Business   4:47

Many feel that the best survival technique for community groups will come from the business community. Financial management and entrepreneurial vision are needed skills.

Corporate Giving: SAFECO   5:00

One Seattle firm is a consistent leader in exercising Corporate Social Responsibility in how it supports communities.

Project Transition   3:47

United Way was already the backbone of most public/private contribution efforts at the local level. This temporary program sought to address transitional needs of non-profit social service providers.

Metrocenter YMCA   5:06
Seattle's most successful grant-seeking organization helped find funding for hundreds of projects and groups. Now it eyes the changing trends of foundation support.

Common Ground   4:10
This housing rehabilitation program takes advantage of support from a special segment of the private sector—churches.

Seattle Emergency Housing   5:02
One reason why Seattle Emergency Housing is expected to survive is its emphasis on providing basic services during hard times. Another is the relationship of the board of directors to the mission of the agency.

The Nature Conservancy   5:00
The oldest and most active land trust in the United States at the time, the Nature Conservancy pitches itself as an investment in the future.

Neighborhood Reinvestment Corporation   5:00
Another group to leverage resources is this national cooperative venture. One local example is Tacoma's Neighborhood Housing Service.

Randolph Carter Industrial Workshop   3:05
This agency boasted of 90 percent self-sufficiency while creating jobs for some most-difficult-to-place clients.

Community Health Clinics   4:40
Seattle already had an innovative system of neighborhood clinics. The groups turned to consortiums to more efficiently provide services.

PART I
The Neighborhoods

Dedication, Voices of Seattle

AO'D: This radio series is dedicated to Seattle and its many communities, from over 100 geographic neighborhoods to literally thousands of associations, auxiliaries, parishes and councils.

Seattle has earned its reputation as a City of Neighborhoods through the work of these groups and the individuals within them. By focusing on the activities of Seattle groups, this series hopes to give some perspective to what has been seen nationally as a "neighborhood movement."

It will attempt to analyze the roles that communities have played and will play in the light of changing political and economic situations. And it tries to put a spotlight on the leaders and role models for community activity in the '80s.

But leaders and role models, while articulate and thought provoking, are only the most visible members of the neighborhood movement.

The true movement is found in those individuals who live, work and play in our communities. And this program would not be complete without presenting some of their voices too. Young and old, they have given their time and effort to making this city more livable by cleaning empty lots or reclaiming valuable waterways.

Child's voice: Well, at first it was really, really, dirty but after we had cleaned it up, it was really clean.

Female voice: If it isn't restored, it's a waste of water, it's a waste of resource, it's a waste of recreation that can be enhanced and can be utilized by the entire North End.

AO'D: From welfare mothers trapped between unemployment and daycare cuts, to middle-class housewives volunteering their time to help.

Female voice: That would mean that he would quite literally have to be alone six or seven hours a day and that's…at 14 months, that's child abuse. [*a child cries*]. They're punishing him. I don't see how you can punish a child.

Other female voice: It's a bunch of moms serving a bunch of kids and other moms and that's how we relate to the families that we're in contact with.

AO'D: From newly arrived Indo-Chinese, looking for freedom and work in a new land, to the low-income person who knows that citizenship is no guarantee of liberty.

Immigrant's voice: I didn't understand because I never see a country, big country like that. I never drive a car. I never see the big building like this. I lived in a small village.

Male voice: They want to put fences—eight-foot fences—and lighting, all around Holly Park to make it look like a concentration camp.

AO'D: From the developers and landlords who honestly believe in the marketplace, to those renters and tenants who have become undesirable obstacles to development.

Male voice: The only way we'll get them out of there is to get them condemned and get the buildings tore down.

Male voice: Tear these down, where the people gonna go?

Female voice: This is my home. All I own is within these four walls. But what's even more important is what about the people that have been here since the '40s? Where are they supposed to go?

AO'D: But most of all, this series is dedicated to those thousands who stood up to work and fight, for their neighborhoods, for their homes, and to have their voices heard.

Female voice: If we don't show them that we care and we want these things done, why should they take their money and do these things?

Older female voice: I ain't got no victory yet, so I don't know what's going to happen. But then I'll tell you the truth, no matter what happens, they're going to have a lawsuit.

In the City of Neighborhoods, I'm Arthur O'Donnell.

The Death of the Neighborhood Movement?

Steve Shepherd: Community councils and community groups certainly had power. They certainly had organizational ability. They certainly had influence. All three. And they accomplished goals. Theoretically, by a community-organizing model, they should have continued to grow. They didn't. In fact, most of them collapsed to a point.

AO'D: Steve Shepherd is a planner with the City of Seattle. For the past 10 years he's been closely involved with community groups and the neighborhood movement. Yet, despite all of the money spent, all of the grass roots organizing done in communities, despite the inclusion of citizen participation in many city decisions, Steve Shepherd says that the neighborhood movement is dead.

He gives several reasons for the movement's demise: that community groups relied too heavily on disappearing government funding, that constant confrontations have driven away officials who otherwise support neighborhood ideals—even the accusation that neighborhood leaders never really represented the interests of their communities.

But most of all, Steve Shepherd feels that neighborhood issues have taken a back seat to larger issues. As proof, he points to the rise of Washington State's energy ratepayer revolt, or the renewal of the Peace Movement.

Steve Shepherd: The single-issue coalition, citywide group became the inheritors of the organizational skill that had been developed through the community councils.

AO'D: Seattle Mayor Charles Royer shares the view that single-issue groups have displaced neighborhood concerns at City Hall.

Royer: And I think that change was driven by the economy. The cost of living in the city, the cost of energy; big issues like big transportation planning, mass transit. Energy became a big issue and out of that now you see the Light Brigade and the Irate Ratepayers. Those groups have displaced, if you will, the Montlake Community Council for attention at City Hall.

AO'D: But whether you see this change as the death of the neighborhood movement, or simply a transition into another phase, pretty much depends on how you initially define the movement.

If you confine it to geographic issues like parking, zoning and street improvements, there is a good reason to assume the neighborhood groups will have less say in government decisions. Simply put, local governments will be moving away from these areas as scarce money is put into other priorities.

Rather, if you see the movement as one of individuals trying to improve their lives and the conditions of those around them, if you recognize the power of organization to make government more responsible, then like Karen Boyle, you recognize the fact that neighborhoods have been the training ground for dealing with problems brought on by a new decade.

Boyle: Suddenly, so quickly—it's incredible to me how things change so quickly—we've seen this great change from the early seventies to the middle seventies to the end, and now going into the eighties.

We've seen these different stages. Three years from now, things could be very different indeed, because of the withdrawal of government support. We are going to have to be more responsible for making sure that social services are available to people in the community. We are taking things into our own hands and there will be other challenges that we will have to rise to, which can be seen as a different role for communities.

AO'D: Perhaps the term "neighborhood movement" is a misnomer for a broader movement that will some day be recognized. Recently, one newspaper article finally revised its assessment of the 1970s, from the "Me Decade" to the "Grassroots Decade." So, there is still hope.

A transition is underway, one that calls for neighbors from every community to recognize the broader needs of the 1980s and to adapt.

Boyle: We would be called to different fronts, and we will be involved in some—as people call it—single-issue issues. It's only obvious that those people who have been on the fronts fighting their community battles will be some of the same people. I think that there will be coalitions where churches and community groups and so forth will be getting together, and we might be needed again.

AO'D: The very same things that brought success to the neighborhood movement—cooperation, confrontation, organization—will be needed for addressing larger issues, as well as an increased political sophistication and an understanding of difficult economic questions. Community groups and the individuals who work with them are willing and able to take on the task.

In the City of Neighborhoods, I'm Arthur O'Donnell.

How Many Communities?

AO'D: Seattle is a place of strong neighborhood identification. When you ask people where they live, they're more likely to name a neighborhood than a street. But even if you knew the names and boundaries of all 113 city neighborhoods, you've only begun to scratch the surface of communities in this city. Steve Shepherd is a city planner, and he breaks down one neighborhood for us.

Shepherd: In the Atlantic neighborhood, I know of Judkin's Community Council, Rejected Community Council, Jackson Place Community Group, Sarah B. Yesler Association, South Atlantic Neighborhood Alliance, and I-90 Concerned Citizens—and an umbrella group that covers four of those six.

AO'D: It would be difficult to take a census of every single community organization in the country and just as difficult to pin a birthdate on organized community activity. But it's widely agreed that in the 20th century, the first surge of community power came from the efforts of social clubs and what were then called local improvement clubs. Terry Pettus is a long-time neighborhood activist. He had his first acquaintanceship with such groups as a reporter for the *Tacoma Ledger* in the 1920s and '30s. Terry says he watched these social clubs take on political and economic roles and then disappear during the Depression.

Pettus: We say that the community clubs in a sense disappeared. Something sprung up called the Unemployed Citizens League, which was a neighborhood organization. I wonder. I can't prove this now, this is purely looking back, did the survival issue transform them from worrying about zoning to worrying about eating?

AO'D: Pettus called these improvement clubs the forerunners of modern community councils. Then, as today, community groups have one basic resource: the individuals who care about their neighborhood and are willing to get involved.

There is no typical neighborhood activist. Each individual has different motives for getting involved. But there is a kind of person that you might expect to find active in any neighborhood, from Seattle to Portland, Maine.

Karen Boyle is just such a person, a wife and mother; she is also the president of the Wallingford Community Council. Karen says she learned the power of organization when a city road improvement directly threatened her home.

Boyle: As an individual I just wasn't going to have the clout that was needed to try to fight something that big. If I really wanted to do anything about it, I should do it through an established organization, through the community council. I soon learned that you just don't turn things over. You've got to roll up your sleeves and be willing to do and to lead.

AO'D: Because there are so many community groups, it's natural that many would join together under a common umbrella to fight for common interests. Jim Diers was an early member of such an umbrella group called SESCO, the Southeast Seattle Community Organization. After three years of organizing individuals around issues, SESCO made the move to representing groups.

Jim Diers: Within a few months we had 23 groups that joined up with SESCO. Just a real impressive array representing every segment of the community.

AO'D: There is another kind of umbrella group that arose directly from federal War on Poverty programs in the 1960s. These multi-service agencies usually represent ethnic minority groups. They fall under the category of community action programs, or CAPs. In Seattle, the oldest is CAMP, Central Area Motivation Program. Walter Hundley was an early director of CAMP, who later went on to become the Superintendent of Parks.

Hundley: The people who were involved in the development CAMP were in most cases also the people who were heavily involved in Civil Rights, and we were able to provide the troops because we had the paid network of people to go out and spread the message.

AO'D: A crucial role in the community movement has been played by non-profit service agencies. In Seattle and King County there are over 1,500 such groups, dealing with special constituencies. More and more, these groups are being asked to provide services to the poor and disadvantaged that government feels it can no longer afford.

Marilyn Chase is the assistant director for the Randolph Carter Industrial Workshop.

Chase: The people we have in here are really the clients of the state, and they purchase our services for their clients. Counseling, evaluation, job training and the like.

AO'D: And finally, there is another type of community group emerging. Some have called it the single-issue group, or public issue advocates. These are not neighborhood-based, but city- or nation-wide. They revolve around a single issue like housing or energy or peace. And while some have called these the death of the neighborhood movement, others see them as a natural step for the community movement to take. Martha Diltz is a housing activist and director of the non-profit agency, Seattle Emergency Housing.

Diltz: I think some of the broadest issues we're facing now are community issues. They're not neighborhood issues. Employment is a community issue. Housing is. Food is. And there need to be alliances that are formed, across town.

In the City of Neighborhoods, I'm Arthur O'Donnell.

What is a Neighborhood?

Karen Boyle: It's being in a small town right in the middle of a big city, and I think that that's what a lot of people feel in their individual neighborhoods. They belong to their neighborhood first, and that neighborhood belongs to the city.

AO'D: It's not easy to precisely define a neighborhood. A city planner might point to geographic boundaries. An academic might determine shared socioeconomic conditions. A politician might see pockets of party affiliation. For Karen Boyle, the definition of the Wallingford neighborhood has taken years of community activism and a couple of terms as its community council president.

The geographic limits of Wallingford—two lakes and two freeways—are easy to identify. In fact, many of Seattle's 113 neighborhoods have easily recognizable boundaries. Many were determined in a 1960's school district study. Other neighborhood's boundaries were physically imposed.

Terry Pettus and residents of the East Lake Community just have to look out their window to see two major borders—Lake Union and Interstate 5.

Pettus: Well, East Lake, in many ways, is a neighborhood that's typical, I'm sure, around the country, where a neighborhood was created by a freeway. Virtually a Chinese wall on one side and a lake on the other.

AO'D: But many neighborhoods are not so easy to define. In Seattle's South End, for instance, few landmarks distinguish borders. Rather, the entire area is defined by a sense of poverty and urban decay. In the early 1970s, a group called SESCO, Southeast Seattle Community Organization, sought to change that problem. According to early member, Jim Diers, the first step in the process was door-to-door canvassing, literally coming up with a neighborhood of common interests.

Diers: Oh, I just knocked on doors and talked to people. Asked them what their problems were, what their concerns were, what they thought about community.

It was usually really small issues that we started with. It was trying to get a stop sign at a dangerous intersection, get a vacant lot cleaned up, trying to get an abandoned house either rehabbed or torn down.

AO'D: More than other Seattle group, SESCO has modeled itself on the ideas of community organizer Saul Alinsky. One basic Alinsky concept is the use of existing community structures—churches and schools—to help define a neighborhood.

Diers: The basic principal of organizing is you start where people are at, and people who are into churches are *really* into churches. They're very committed to them; that's their community. I think oftentimes it's a more natural community than the neighborhood because the neighborhood's gone through such incredible transitions over the years. Some people continue to come to their church even though they've moved out to the suburbs. The churches have a strong interest in being good for the community and being a part of the community, which fits in exactly with what organizing is all about.

AO'D: When an organization like SESCO tries to align itself with neighbors, it finds success when it deals with small issues. According to Jim Diers, SESCO's earliest victory came about this way: A neighborhood school was located on a busy street. When a serious accident injured two children, the residents joined together to request streetlights and stop signs from the city. But this particular intersection was not a high priority for the engineering department.

Diers: Finally, we just decided we'd exercise our pedestrian rights. There was a group of 75 people that got organized. They just used the crosswalk, back and forth, back and forth, stopping all traffic on Empire Way. It wasn't long after that that they got their signal light.

AO'D: Neighborhoods are likely to organize in opposition to something—a high-rise apartment, a school closure, a freeway. Activists are quick to point out that such threats transcend the differences among neighbors.

Boyle: It doesn't matter what kind of education you have or who you are, whenever there's a crisis in Wallingford, all kinds of people come pouring out to help. When there's no crisis going on, it seems that the people are complacent. But that isn't true. Just threaten to put in a high rise or take out a school or what have you. and the people are there, all kinds of people.

AO'D: But threats are not the only organizing tool. Often, Seattle residents have found their neighborhood identity by working together for positive ends. Terry Pettus is a retired president of the Floating Home Owners Association. He recalls how a park clean-up project brought people in his neighborhood together.

Pettus: When we were working down there, an old man, a retired senior, was living up there in a little apartment. He saw all this activity and he came down and wanted to know what he could do. And lo and behold he fixed up this sign—"Welcome to Lynn Street Park." Well, he's long dead but his sign is still there. And it seems to me that it's a symbolism of how communities are built. They're built with people and relationships between people.

In the City of Neighborhoods, I'm Arthur O'Donnell.

Roots of the Neighborhood Movement

Steve Shepherd: A whole series of things came together. You had Model Cities organizing the core of the Central Area. You had the city coming in through the Neighborhood Improvement Program, organizing some of the peripheral neighborhoods. And you had the issue of R.H. Thompson uniting some of the areas along the path. And suddenly, we had what appeared to be a huge grassroots spring into being. People began to say, "Wow, there's a neighborhood movement!"

AO'D: There, in a nutshell is the birth of Seattle's neighborhood movement. According to city planner, Steve Shepherd, three issues came together almost simultaneously—helping to set the tone of neighborhood organization for a decade.

The three were the federal Model Cities program, Neighborhood Improvement Projects funded through a local bond proposal called forward thrust and finally, the opposition to a highway project, the R.H. Thompson Expressway. In a sense, all of these events came about as a result of government policies.

The Model Cities Program was an outgrowth of the Great Society. It brought a host of federal resources into a handful of cities and helped make minority communities a political power. Walter Hundley, now Seattle's Superintendent of Parks, was the director of Seattle's Model City project in 1968.

Hundley: The idea was to throw great gobs of money at this problem of ghetto neighborhoods—surround them with all kinds of resources, you know, get the whole shmear!

AO'D: Looking back the goals of Model Cities—to wipe out urban problems—seemed far beyond the financial and political capability of any federal program.

But Seattle's project can claim a major success in formalizing the process of involving ordinary citizens in identifying problems and trying to come up with solutions to them. According to Walter Hundley, that's a far cry from the days when Seattle's minorities looked to one or two leaders to be their representatives.

Hundley: They were the ones that people came to us and said, "Go downtown *for* us and tell them what's wrong." Now, they all stream in here. I don't think we would have had the strong community council, community club movement that we have now without Model Cities really setting the pace.

AO'D: Another local government effort that had significant impact on neighborhoods was the Forward Thrust bond issue. In 1968, King County voters approved a massive $120 million bond issue to buy parkland and to make capital improvements in communities. At that time, according to Steve Shepherd, 22 community councils managed to win access to about $10 million of that money for use in their neighborhoods.

Shepherd: They had a tool—money—to give them legitimacy to their own constituency. They had staff assistance from the city to help them with publicity and so they became stronger. Of course, they've become stronger.

AO'D: And this leads to an interesting paradox inherent to the neighborhood movement. For very often the issues that excited neighborhood groups brought them into direct conflict with the government agencies that helped them organize. And in city after city, one issue arose that brought a clash between neighborhoods and government—the construction of a freeway. In Seattle, it was the R.H. Thompson Expressway.

Shepherd: A freeway is always a wonderful organizing tool. Things can be drawn in black and white, very much bad and good. And the freeway is bad and no freeway is good—very clear strategy, and a challenge and a threat. Well, obviously, R.H. Thompson was a direct threat.

Terry Pettus is a long-time Seattle activist. He says he uses the example of the expressway to show how communities get organized. In this case, the movement began when a college professor opened his newspaper one morning.

Pettus: Well, the damn thing is coming right through his house. And he got very much concerned and got on the phone, called some friends and had them over for coffee. And that's how that movement started. One person got concerned and contacted neighbors and started a movement, which I think was the first time that a freeway—that was already on the map—was scrubbed.

Another Seattleite with a long-term prospective on the neighborhood movement is Mayor Charles Royer. As a TV newsman, Royer watched and reported on the growing neighborhood movement. Then, in the mid-1970s, he made the move into politics, successfully running on a neighborhood-oriented platform. Now as mayor, Royer often is confronted by the demands of community activists.

Royer: Something happens when you have a good achievement, like having stopped a freeway. There's a sense of achievement and there's a sense of joy of having been in it. It was fun, it was exciting, it was meaningful, important—all of those good values are, you know, driving people to stay in that. They're kind of looking for some more attention.

AO'D: During the 1970s, Seattle's neighborhood groups had no lack of battles to fight. And it's apparent that many of the same concerns will exist in the '80s.

Recently the city and county announced a new bond proposal. Some call it the "Son of Forward Thrust." Another freeway project, the completion of Interstate 90, is one of the hottest issues in town.

The problems of inner cities remain. They're now a target of President Reagan's Urban Enterprise Zones. What role neighborhood groups will play in handling these issues is still the question.

In the City of Neighborhoods, I'm Arthur O'Donnell.

Tactics

Jim Diers: What the press picks up on is always the exciting event, the confrontation.

AO'D: This is Jim Diers. He worked for years as a community organizer for Southeast Seattle Community Organization. SESCO was set up on a model based on the teachings of organizer Saul Alinsky. The group has often been accused of using confrontations to get its way, but Diers feels such tactics are justified.

Diers: SESCO's never started with confrontations. A key principle of Alinsky organizing is you start where the people are at. And where the people are at right at first is to write those letters, to get those petitions in, to meet with officials, to try to work things out. Only when those things fail, people take some kind of stronger action.

AO'D: The most common form of confrontation is a demonstration around a single issue, and SESCO has sponsored more than a few. One that Diers recalls was to draw attention to the dangers of the Lucille Street Bridge, a turn-of-the-century wooden structure, which clearly could not handle modern traffic. It took a seven-year-long struggle for residents to finally get a new bridge—a struggle marked by negotiation breakdowns, failed promises and, on one sunny afternoon, a parade across the bridge.

Diers: And it was just incredible. There were 600 people there. People, who had never marched before in their lives, never really been that involved before, came out in droves, angry. We had the bowling league there. They came with their bowling balls and bowling bags. We had the soccer teams come up, the kids in their uniforms. There was a guy in an RV camper that led the whole demonstration. He had a bullhorn attached to the top of his house, playing music, "Lucille Street Bridge is coming down." Five city council people were in that march with us and were just really impressed.

AO'D: Confrontations are not only used to bring about change. And neighbors can fight just as hard to keep things the way they are.

Mary Lynn Myer: To stick to the status quo is always the starting point for anyone. Sometimes it is also a strategy that if one sticks to the status quo, one won't have to accept as much change as if one agreed to go with the change. You don't have to make a lot of decisions.

AO'D: Seattle city planner, Mary Lynn Meyer, recalls her first community organizing experience, preparing a small town for the intrusion of a federal dam-building project. One home that stood in the way housed an ailing elderly woman, whose doctor said she did not have long to live.

Meyer: No one wanted to relocate her. It was sure that if she were to leave her house that she'd probably, you know, not make it. However, the construction schedule was such that her home was scheduled to be torn down within two weeks. The confrontation tactic that was used was simply to stand in front of the house *en masse* when the bulldozers came. And, of course, it worked.

AO'D: As president of the Wallingford Community Council, Karen Boyle has fought many battles with city departments. But, she says, her biggest victory could not have been without the help of the city. Increasingly, Wallingford residents were the victims of crime, and neighbors were tired of living under siege.

Boyle: It's the first time I started out with something really in a positive way. I certainly remember the day that I woke up and said, "Wait a minute! If I can fight schools being closed and highways from coming through the neighborhood, I can fight burglars too!"

AO'D: After a year, the Wallingford Watch Program is considered one of the most successful in the nation, involving 200 block-watch captains and 4,500 homes. But it would not have gotten off the ground if Wallingford neighbors were unwilling to cooperate with police officials and bureaucratic methods.

The use of confrontation tactics has long been a dividing point among community organizers. But it should be obvious that neighborhood groups never rely solely on either cooperation or confrontation. They use each according to the situation.

Terry Pettus learned his organizing through trade-union activities and later with neighborhood groups. He says clearly not every issue demands a strike or a confrontation.

Pettus: So you can get a lot of publicity through certain types of confrontation. But what do you want? Do you want to accomplish something?

AO'D: Whenever possible, Pettus counsels cooperation with authorities because there will always be another battle to fight and then you might need the help of someone you've opposed in the past.

Pettus: Neighborhood groups have to be a little more sophisticated politically. And remember, always remember in politics and public affairs that you don't have enemies, you have adversaries. You don't have friends, you have allies.

In the City of Neighborhoods, I'm Arthur O'Donnell.

Central Area Motivation Program

AO'D: When the Community Service Administration closed its doors last October, it marked the end of an era. In 1964 CSA began life as the Office of Economic Opportunity. It served as the funnel for millions of federal dollars to urban neighborhoods. Programs like Head Start, Job Corps, Vista and Upward Bound all had their home at CSA.

The office was also a major funder of community action programs, multi-service agencies that served low-income neighborhoods. In Seattle, the oldest and largest of these is CAMP, the Central Area Motivation Program. As it has since the mid-60s, it occupies an old firehouse in a minority neighborhood. During 1981, CAMP received $440,000 in CSA money. When the federal agency closed down, some of its budget was transformed into state-administered block grants, but the dollar reduction was substantial. CAMP's 1982 allocation dropped to $270,000. Next year, CAMP's director Larry Gossett expects only $81,000.

Gossett: When you go from 40 staff to two-and-a-half staff in a two-year period, that's almost impossible to maintain any kind of basic operation that could provide multi-services.

AO'D: CAMP is a prime example of just how the changes in federal policy have affected community groups. In the early 1960s, the Democratic administration was beginning to turn its attention to long-neglected urban problems. In Seattle, CAMP was set up to tap into this new source of money.

Gossett: I think we got money because we had a really broad base and representative group, and the people in the leadership were smart enough to get people who were really able to help them put together good proposals.

AO'D: Even as the abundance of federal dollars helped CAMP to grow and prosper, it also bred dependency. Walter Hundley was an early director of CAMP who later went on to head the Seattle Model Cities program and then become the city's Superintendent of Parks. From his office in City Hall, Hundley looks back over the years with one regret, that he was unable to complete an early effort to make CAMP self-sufficient.

Hundley: We had established a track record of being able to attract federal money and even state money like crazy. I could see that that was going to end one day. I didn't know just when but I knew one day it was. I worked fairly closely with the Jewish Community Center people when they still had their offices downtown here, and I would watch their fund drives over the years and how that money grew and how they built that beautiful thing over east of the lake. And here's CAMP, still sitting in the firehouse, looking for federal money.

AO'D: In the years since Hundley's departure, CAMP has experienced many successes and failures. At one point a director left office in a hurry. CAMP's low-income weatherization program had become the focus of what Seattle's media called a "funding scandal." That's when Larry Gossett stepped in, instituting a rigid policy of financial accountability.

Gossett: Much of the problem had been with poor management, not necessarily embezzlement or fraud, just poor management—not having enough staff or the kind of staff that are able to identify problems and come up with corrective ways of doing away with those problems. We at CAMP have been very successful at putting together a fiscal management system that all of our funding sources think is good and responsible.

AO'D: But dependency on federal dollars remained. In the past few years CAMP has lost much of its financial report, including all of its CETA [Community Employment & Training Agency] workers, its fund-raising staff and its volunteer coordinators.

It's sad to say that CAMP has not developed very many strategies for survival. Larry Gossett says the cuts came too fast and hard to develop meaningful alternatives.

One big hope lies in the development of an untapped economic resource. Unlike the rest of Seattle, the Central Area is unserved by cable television. Currently, many large cable companies are hoping to win city council approval for developing this potentially lucrative section of town. CAMP and other community groups have made a deal with one of the competitors—their support in the franchise hearings in return for a 10 percent ownership and channel access.

Gossett: Our coalition of groups, over the life of the franchise, will have $2.5 to $3 million returned to the community. We will have ownership in the company that by the end of the life of the franchise—15 years—will be worth another $2 million dollars.

AO'D: If CAMP is to survive, it must first shed its dependency on government funding, then build a new constituency in the Central Area. If it doesn't survive, its demise will simply mark the end of an era.

In the City of Neighborhoods, I'm Arthur O'Donnell.

The City and Neighborhoods

Steve Shepherd: Government, as far as I'm concerned, has manipulated the community movement to its own ends. We got to be very good at appearances. We'd schedule our meetings in rooms that were a little bit smaller than, you know, you think you would need. The media would come and what they'd see would be a packed room, with 250 residents. What they'd failed to realize is that the neighborhood had 10,000 residents.

AO'D: It is perhaps ironic that Seattle holds a national reputation for encouraging community involvement in planning. According to Steve Shepherd, it's been five years since the city treated neighborhoods as a high priority.

Shepherd: All the state and city goals were to support the community growth, the community participation. The city made—as far as I can see—a very conscious decision not to do that anymore and to begin to plan on a citywide basis and not take community councils into account.

AO'D: After 11 years of city planning, Steve Shepherd and the Office of Neighborhood Technical Assistance have undergone many changes.

With the rise of the neighborhood movement, an Office of Neighborhood Planning was set up in the city's Department of Community Development. At that time, ONP's job was to act as liaison between the city and federal Community Action Programs like Model Cities. Under the terms of the 1968 Forward Thrust bond issue, ONP's job was to help organize community councils, to create neighborhood improvement plans and to decide on spending priorities.

Throughout the 1970s organizing remained an important task for ONP. With the growth of block grant funds, low and moderate-income neighborhoods were given a chance to decide how money would be spent. That money, and the attention provided by city planners gave neighborhood groups a legitimacy in dealing with other government offices.

But some feel the desires of neighborhoods and community councils too often conflicted with the policies of the mayor and the city council. Neighborhood Planning's role was changed from organizing neighborhoods to becoming a mediator in issues concerning communities. Even its name was changed recently to the Office of Neighborhood Technical Assistance. This reflects a less activist role.

Now there are even greater changes in the wind. Funding cutbacks affect every American city; Seattle is no different. Rumors in City Hall talk about the possible closure of Neighborhood Technical Assistance, a rumor not denied by Mayor Charles Royer.

Royer: I'm not sure that we can get any further into the business of assisting in organization of neighborhood groups. If the choice comes down to the Office of Neighborhood Planning and patrol strength on the street for police, we'll go with the police, if we get down to a level that is seen to be dangerous.

AO'D: Mary Lynn Myer is also a planner for the city. She says she recognizes the changes in her office as an indication of the times. Seattle will spend less time and effort in helping neighborhoods organize.

Myer: If those neighborhoods that have not yet gone through an organizing phase have something happen to them, lots of times they don't know what to do. It's a chaotic situation for them. They run around trying to find information, trying to find avenues of action, feeling frustrated, feeling alienated.

AO'D: As you might expect, the changes in city policy towards neighborhoods and citizen participation might tend to breed frustration among activists and city bureaucrats.

Myer: Boy, you look back on them and you say, "That was a lot of time. That was a lot of my energy. I went to all those meetings. I hassled through all those discussions with all of those people, and we arrived at some conclusions. And the studies are done and then they're put on the shelf. And what has happened because of them?" So it tends to make one feel a little bit more cynical.

AO'D: Both the Mayor and Mary Lynn Myer are quick to point out values that have grown from the neighborhood movement. Royer points to examples of neighborhood action to help come up with solutions for difficult problems, like traffic and parking near a ferry terminal, or the location of low-income housing in a middle-class neighborhood.

Royer: In both cases, neighborhood organizations came up with a positive and good solution. I surely see neighborhood groups as positive instruments of change on, still, those neighborhood-specific or geographic-specific issues.

Myer: Obviously, the good is that people *have* been able to get together. They know what arguments hold weight with the system, what arguments don't hold weight, who to call within the system, who *not* to call, where to go for information and even, tactically speaking, what tactics bring the most results.

AO'D: The Office of Neighborhood Technical Assistance is in transition. How it fares over the next few months will be an indication of Seattle's future commitment to neighborhoods.

In the City of Neighborhoods, I'm Arthur O'Donnell.

New Federalism—Block Grants

AO'D: When President Reagan took office he declared a New Federalism, actually a de-federalization of programs and revenue sources. The goal was to cut the size of the central bureaucracy and to increase the responsibilities of state and local governments in funding social programs. One example in Seattle has been the de-federalization of the Public Health Service. Director Richard Tompkins says there's nothing new about the New Federalism.

Tompkins: And the Reagan budget proposal was the Nixon proposal from '73; I mean, they took it out of the filing cabinets and dusted it off.

AO'D: Although the New Federalism has run into some serious roadblocks in Congress and in governors' offices, it has already an effect on cities and community organizations.

Larry Gossett: As an anti-poverty, multi-purpose social service agency, we have been very reliant upon public sources for our support. So, when there was a radical shift in the federal outlook, that had a big impact on our funding and our program support.

AO'D: That's Larry Gossett, director of the Seattle Central Area Motivation Program. CAMP is one of 28 community action programs in Washington State, which used to get funding from the Community Service Administration. CSA began life as the Great Society's Office of Economic Opportunity. It was the home of Vista, Head Start and dozens of other community-oriented programs.

When CSA closed its doors in October 1981, about half of its budget was turned into community service block grants and given to the state for administration.

Although $8 million suddenly became $4 million, Governor John Spellman of Washington welcomed the opportunity to assume state responsibility for the program.

Spellman: It exists and it's an opportunity. I just felt if we fell into the usual rhetoric of carping, as is going on around the rest of the country, then we would lose time and, perhaps more importantly, lose the togetherness which we already had.

AO'D: However, it's apparent other government officials are not as optimistic about the effects of state take-over. This is Charles Royer, the Mayor of Seattle.

Royer: We have a great example on the Interstate System. It was a national purpose to build the Interstate Highway System; it was decided at that time to let the states do the maintenance. They did it in such a spotty and sporadic way that now, much of the federal gas tax revenues are going into major rebuilding of the Interstate System, because it's been allowed to fail. I think if programs like housing, mass transit—all of the social programs that have built up over the last 30-40 years—if those are allowed to fall into the kind of disrepair that the Interstate System has through state lack of support, then we've lost a great deal.

AO'D: The issue of block grants is a major concern for Royer. In 1981, Seattle received over $16 million in Community Development Block Grants from the federal Department of Housing and Urban Development. The Community Development Block Grant program was a major part of Richard Nixon's "revenue sharing" and it's had a significant effect on communities around the nation. First of all, it helped give cities a direct link to federal administrators. Secondly, block grant money was often passed on to neighborhood groups for local improvements, and to non-profit groups to pay for social service operations.

So far, Community Development Block Grants have not been the object of state takeover, but Mayor Royer worries about the future of cities if that should happen and suburban-dominated legislatures assume control of the funding.

Royer: That would be a great departure from history if we were to get a reasonable hearing in the state Legislature.

AO'D: Community organizers are very concerned over the future of block grants, but for different reasons. Jim Diers spent years organizing Seattle's South End communities so they could win a piece of block grant funds. He feels that block grants have often been used as a way to co-opt neighborhood groups. And now Diers sees another risk.

Diers: The block grant program basically is not a way to transfer power to the local community, but rather it's a mechanism to transfer funds from social programs to military.

AO'D: Aside from the reallocation of money away from social spending, states relying on block grant funds have reported unstable cash flow from the federal government with as much as a two-month delay in funding agencies. This is compounded by many states' own budgetary problems, which preclude them from picking up funding for community action programs.

In fact, if there are lessons to be learned from President Nixon's revenue sharing, it is that states will likely use block grant funds to address their own budget crises rather than maintain federal programs for communities.

In the City of Neighborhoods, I'm Arthur O'Donnell.

Public Health Hospital

AO'D: It stands at the north end of Beacon Hill, like a symbol of Franklin Roosevelt's New Deal. Seattle Public Health Hospital rose during the depths of the Great Depression. At first a hospital for merchant marines, Public Health has seen its role and use change radically during the years. Like the government that built it, it got larger, added new programs and worked down into the poorest of communities.

Now, as one outgrowth of President Reagan's New Federalism, the Public Health Hospital is no longer a part of the federal government. Instead, it is a municipal cooperative, run by the community, and responsible for its own financial survival. Dr. Richard Tompkins is the director of Seattle Public Health. He says that every president since Richard Nixon has tried to close that facility.

Tompkins: The major closure attempt that occurred in the Nixon administration had a very sizeable impact on this institution in two regards. First of all, I think it made a lot of people realize how frail the institution was in a political sense. Because they realized that, a lot of people banded together into a coalition to keep the hospital as a federal institution, and that particular coalition of community people and political people has persisted.

AO'D: Attorney Bob Kaplan was one member of the coalition seeking to keep Public Health alive in Seattle. Both he and Tompkins tell of a large difference between the administration's rhetoric of turning the hospital to community control, and what they see as the real intent.

Kaplan: Turning over to community control was in reality, "Let's close the hospitals." There was no real substantial expectation that the hospitals would, in fact, transition into community facilities.

Tompkins: Secretary [Richard] Schweiker's [Health and Human Services] department was doing everything in its power to shut this institution down and not allow the transition to occur. They didn't want to be bothered with it. They saw a straw man all of a sudden become alive, and that was not they wanted.

AO'D: In the 1970s the Public Health system was kept alive mostly through the efforts of Washington State's Senator Warren Magnussen. One Magnussen bill commissioned the National Health Service Corps and allowed the Public Health Hospital to provide back-up care for clients of Seattle's community clinics. By the time that Reagan's proposal threatened closure, Public Health had become so vital to Seattle's health care system that the city led the move towards community transition. This is Seattle Mayor Charles Royer.

Royer: It was not only the city that got involved in this. The city was a major political actor and a major actor in the transition, but private medicine found it in their best interest to keep the hospital open. The cost of health care is a cost on everybody. Every time the cost of health care goes up that's added on to the cost of goods or added on to the cost of delivering a service, so there was a mutual self-interest and a decent self-interest in this community to save the hospital.

AO'D: In October of 1981 the battle was over. Although cut off from federal operating funds, Public Health had won a $26 million block grant for capital improvements. According to Dr. Tompkins, that's nearly twice as much money as had been put into the facility in its 50 years of federal life. But the job of transition remained.

Tompkins: Getting the hospital going from a federal institution, which was just getting regular checks from the federal government, to set up a billing system, to set up all kinds of different patient accounting systems than the federal government used, has been a full-time job. The only thing that he didn't change was the clinical practice. We kept all of our doctors, we kept all of our non-physician professional staff, and they kept seeing patients right through this thing. We didn't lose a single minute of patient care time. And, from the standpoint of our patients, the important thing that they noticed is that the institution is improving.

AO'D: Despite city and state backing for community control, Public Health can expect no funds from these government bodies. Instead, it must stand on its own ability to attract patients for its services.

Tompkins: Letting people know that the hospital is open and available to serve the public and anyone that wants to come to the hospital can come. There's physicians up there that can be primary care physicians for people.

AO'D: Still, Dr. Tompkins states flatly that inability to pay will not bar anyone from receiving care at Public Health.

Tompkins: The finances will not ever be a barrier to access up here, as long as we can keep the doors open.

AO'D: The role that Public Health plays is not unique to Seattle's health care system. On April 1st, the Baltimore Public Health Hospital followed in Seattle's footsteps towards community control. Dr. Tompkins and his staff, as well as all of their supporters throughout the city, feel that the Public Health Hospital has a very important lesson to teach medical facilities everywhere.

Tompkins: It's an approach to care that we think is efficient, is effective; [it] does great things for you professionally if you happen to be the professional, does great things for you clinically if you happen to be the patient; is in my opinion the wave of the future. Because it's efficient, it's also the economic way of the future.

In the City of Neighborhoods, I'm Arthur O'Donnell.

The Home of the Good Shepherd

AO'D: Some have suggested that the neighborhood movement never really existed, that community councils accomplished little and that non-profits will close their doors when government funding disappears.

But to prove this is untrue, one only has to walk behind the tall hedges and iron wrought fence of the Good Shepherd Center.

Built in 1906 as a Catholic home for wayward girls, the building occupies 11½ acres of park and orchard at the crest of Wallingford Hill. It also occupies an important chapter in the story of Seattle's neighborhood movement. In the early 1970s, the Catholic Church decided that the Good Shepherd Center was expendable, and it was closed down.

The building could have been demolished and the land turned over to condominium or shopping center development. Instead, it was saved by a combination of the efforts of citizens, organizations and the city, preserved as a community center and park.

This is Karen Boyle, former Wallingford Community Council president.

Boyle: A lot of groups, a lot of people worked hard for years to make sure that that would be kept in the community as it is—the building and the land.

AO'D: A Sunday afternoon visitor to the Good Shepherd Center might be lucky enough to stumble on a neighborhood party. The occasion was the dedication of a new bandstand at Meridian Park behind the Center, and the whole community got involved. The Senior Center made the hot dogs, the arts community provided entertainment, and local businesses gave away prizes.

This is Wallingford's honorary mayor, Victor Lygdman.

Lygdman: Actually, I went out on 45th and Wallingford one morning at 6:00 a.m., and I said, "I am The Mayor." I didn't hear a voice of dissent so I declared myself official Mayor of Wallingford. As Honorary Mayor, naturally I would be M.C. at the bandstand ceremony, and we wanted to inaugurate it properly so we pulled out all the stops and got all the music and food we could here.

AO'D: From the pea patches of the neighborhood garden to the solar greenhouses of Tilth's Urban Agriculture Project, from recess at the Montessori Day School to the Senior Center's Sunday pancake breakfasts, the Good Shepherd Center is bursting with life and purpose.

AO'D: Twice a month, the Wallingford Senior Center puts on a special meal, a Sunday pancake breakfast and a Tuesday night spaghetti feed to help raise money for their rent and their activities.

Senior voice: Naturally, the government's cutting down and cutting back and cutting back, and we've got to raise a little bit of extra money. So this is our way of doing it.

AO'D: The Good Shepherd Center is operated by the non-profit organization Historic Seattle, which rents out space in the building to arts groups and community organizations. The rent paid by these groups helps keep the Center in operation.

One group housed at the Good Shepherd Center is the Seattle branch of Greenpeace, the internationally known environmental activist organization. Julie McCullough says that rents at the Good Shepherd Center are comparatively low, but the returns for being there are great.

McCullough: Historic Seattle believes that these old buildings like the Good Shepherd Center shouldn't be preserved just for aesthetic purposes but rather they should somehow pay their way if they're going to be preserved. And we like the idea of being in a community center like this.

AO'D: Seattle's Greenpeace is another example of a non-profit group whose fundraising efforts are a model for other groups around the country. McCullough coordinates activities like the Annual Walk for Whales and this past year's Radiothon co-sponsored by KZAM radio. Each of these activities raised over $50,000 for Greenpeace.

McCullough: A lot of people come to me and say, "How is it that you guys do it? How is that you make all this money on these things? We've tried it and we just don't make it." Whenever we have an event, we try to do something more for the person that's giving us money than just giving them a warm feeling in their stomach that they've given to Greenpeace—whether it's a membership card and a subscription to a national magazine. Or, like with the Radiothon, people got a chance to win speakers, and floral arrangements, and dinners, and hot tubs, and all kinds of things like that where the business gave it to Greenpeace. When we sold it, the money came to Greenpeace and it was an all-win situation because the person that won it usually wanted to buy that kind of an item anyway.

AO'D: Greenpeace, the Pacific Northwest Ballet, the Grey Panthers, the Factory School of Visual Arts, Tilth, the Wallingford Community Council and all other renters of the Good Shepherd Center have an advisory role in the operation of the building.

Karen Boyle says one of the big issues facing renters is future development of unused building space.

Boyle: There are 30,000 square feet that are undeveloped—the third, fourth and fifth floors, and how those will be used will have a lot to do with defining what kind of a building that is.

AO'D: Inside and out, the Good Shepherd Center is a visible reminder of the positive effects of the neighborhood movement in Seattle.

It stands as a symbol of cooperation between the city, individuals and non-profit community agencies to serve the needs of neighborhood residents. And through the innovative projects of its tenants, it is proof positive that the neighborhood movement will last long into the 1980's.

In the City of Neighborhoods, I'm Arthur O'Donnell.

PART II

Non-Profit Survival Guide

Thinking Like a Business

AO'D: The studies and reports are beginning to come in, and the headlines reflect their findings:

"Budget reductions pose a threat to the survival of non-profit groups."

"Corporate contributions fail to keep pace with the cuts."

"Social service agency closes its doors."

At the very same time, we could be hearing headlines like:

"Groups find new survival strategies."

"Agency reaches self-sufficiency."

Both sets of headlines are equally true. These are difficult times for organizations. Many may not survive. But many are meeting the challenges. And some are even thriving. They are doing it by bolstering their physical management, by using sophisticated financial techniques, and in some cases, by starting business enterprises to replace lost revenues.

Loren Cole: These kinds of techniques are absolutely essential if you want to survive, if you want to grow, and if you want to deliver good services to your clients.

AO'D: Loren Cole is director of Inquiring Systems, Incorporated. He travels the country, teaching non-profit groups the techniques of survival.

Cole: How to do a cost analysis, how to do cash flow statements, how to be more conscientious about the ways in which you identify what your expectations are of people, and their expectations of you.

AO'D: Cole is not alone in his quest to turn non-profits into entrepreneurs.

A recent study by the Neighborhood Development Collaborative points out the need for business-like solutions to funding problems. That's wise advice according to Loren Cole. Even groups which look to corporations for charitable donations would benefit from a business-like approach.

Cole: A business plan approach talks specifically about outcomes and how they're generated and they look at cash flow, they look at operating statements, that look at, you've done a market survey, you determine the extent of the need. It's very, very concrete.

AO'D: But Cole says he would like to see non-profits break away from dependence on grants and contributions and develop new sources of funding. The first and most obvious is to begin charging for some services provided to clients.

Cole: You might see an alcohol recovery program, which maybe takes $600 a month to service one person who is trying to recover from alcoholism, and they can only charge them maybe $250. So they charge a partial fee, $250 of the $600 they need and then they raise the money elsewhere. That's called revenue-generating services.

AO'D: Of course, not all non-profits can or should charge their clients for services. Another trend in revenue generating might be termed "related-business development."

Cole: Stick with the alcohol recovery program, for example. Now maybe you have homes where people come, the alcoholics live there. And so now you get into a business maybe which goes in and you recondition a building, a home, and then you resell it and you make a profit on it. Now the building, process, of rehabilitating it, is actually a work/therapy program for the alcoholic people who are working there. So this benefits your service. At the same time that's going to subsidize your program, so that's called a related-business development.

AO'D: There is now more emphasis on unrelated-business development, also called "arms-length development". This could take any number of forms. A simple example might be the investment procedures followed by non-profit foundation's endowment portfolio.

Cole: The foundation is investing its endowment in profit-making firms. It generates income on an annual basis. That income's used to provide me with grants.

AO'D: Finally, Loren Cole points out that one of the most effective ways for non-profits to better manage themselves and their resources is to look into the idea of merging, or at least thinking about forming under the umbrella of a consortium.

Cole: What we need are organizational consortiums, which provide management expertise. They help in the marketing, they can use computer systems for physical operations, they can ensure more cost-effective, more efficient ways of working. They can purchase supplies by volume discounts and therefore assist in maintaining cost-effective ways of operating for non-profits.

AO'D: These strategies for economic survival are exciting and workable, and this series has tried to point out specific Seattle examples of how these ideas can be put to use. But simply grafting business ideas onto a non-profit group structure could be disastrous. Another critical issue is whether a group's staff and board members have the necessary skills and training to make sound business decisions.

Those which do, stand a better chance of surviving the 1980s.

In the City of Neighborhoods, I'm Arthur O'Donnell.

Corporate Giving—SAFECO

Stan Karson: You do business best in a well-balanced community, and that's what the marketplace should be like. If the marketplace is burdened with many kinds of problems, the ability to do business in it also suffers.

AO'D: Because of federal funding cutbacks to many social and health services, there has been a lot of talk of an increased dependence on donations by corporations.

While it's unrealistic to assume that corporate efforts could even approach filling the gaps, it is apparent that more companies are looking for ways to exercise what might be called their "corporate social responsibility."

There is one industry that seems to stand out in its efforts to aid American communities. Since 1968, the Life and Health Insurance Industry Association has been making a concerted effort to find solutions to urban problems. At that time, some large eastern insurance companies pledged $2 million to help rebuild communities wrecked by urban decay.

Since then the focus has continued, closely monitored by an industry group called the Clearing House for Corporate Social Responsibility. Stan Karson is the Clearinghouse director.

Karson: What affects the stability of American society and the stability of its communities, its towns and cities, affects the insurance business. We're talking about self-interest.

AO'D: One of Seattle's largest companies is the SAFECO Insurance Company. SAFECO has established itself as a leader, both in charitable contributions and in developing community-based programs.

Back in 1979, SAFECO's board of directors embarked on a program for increasing the company's financial contributions to non-profit organizations. Each year, the percentage of pre-tax profits the company contributes has risen. By 1983, that level will reach 2 percent, translating into approximately $2 million in donations.

John Gilleland is a community relations officer for SAFECO. He says the emphasis on contributions from profits represents a major change in corporate policy.

Gilleland: Going back probably to the time the company was founded in 1923, you've probably found corporate philanthropy to be the business of the chief executive of the company. For a long time, there probably was a philosophy that that was not the role of a corporation, to take its profit and put it out into the community on a programmed basis. You can make a case that profit belonged to the shareholders, or to the employees who helped earn it, or to the customers of your company, any company, in the form of reduced costs.

AO'D: In determining the amount of money available for contributions each year, SAFECO uses an averaging formula, spreading its profit figures over five years to help smooth out any large fluctuations, which might occur because of business downturns. This averaging gives a welcomed stability to the contributions program.

Mary Malarky is SAFECO's contributions manager. She says the company has traditionally held a special interest in insurance-related issues like health and safety programs.

Malarky: That, I see as my responsibility, to weed out those things that are not well managed, those things which are not appropriate for SAFECO to support and to push those things that are appropriate, that are good.

AO'D: But in times of urgent need, priorities are shifting. SAFECO has set up a special response fund to address areas especially hit by cutbacks and begun a project devoted to decreasing youth unemployment.

Malarky: I think you'll find that our philosophy is that in times of emergencies such as we're facing now—times of great change—that the highest priority will go to the organizations that are dealing with direct service to someone in need.

AO'D: Many companies report that they are being flooded with funding requests from frantic non-profits that are searching for alternative sources. But, according to Mary Malarky, SAFECO's requests are holding steady, and because of a well-thought-out contributions policy, groups know exactly what SAFECO's interests are.

Malarky: So, I'm getting better proposals. I'm getting proposals that really understand our guidelines and our areas of emphasis.

AO'D: Charitable contributions are not the only resource a company can offer. SAFECO has begun an extensive employee volunteer program, and its community relations department often provides services like printing to help publicize neighborhood activities.

Dollar for dollar, there is no way the corporate community can make up for federal cuts. The 1981 contribution figures show a half-billion dollar increase. Balance that against $40 billion in federal cuts.

But companies like SAFECO are showing that hometown corporations do have a role to play.

In the City of Neighborhoods, I'm Arthur O'Donnell.

Project Transition

AO'D: Last year American business contributed $3 billion to non-profit organizations. In normal times, such an amount would be hailed as stupendous, marvelous, and a great showing of corporate social responsibility. Unfortunately these are not normal times, and a half-billion dollar increase in contributions seems lost amid the multiple billions of direct federal cutbacks to social services.

At budget-cutting time, there was a great deal of rhetoric concerning the ability of the private sector to fill the gaps. But because of the continued recession, the latest contribution figures have shown that American business is in no position to solve the problem. That does not mean that business isn't trying. In fact, lean times seem to have brought out some very special efforts on the part of the private sector. In Seattle, one of these efforts is called the Project Transition. Peter Maurer is project manager.

Maurer: We realize that with the very abrupt changes that were being taken in support of social and health service programs that there would be a lot of people who would fall between the cracks and would virtually have nowhere else to turn.

AO'D: Project Transition was set up under the wing of the King County United Way as a way to identify the groups and people who would be most affected by government cuts. Instead of setting up a new fundraising agency, Maurer says that affiliation with United Way provided an immediate credibility and an established network of resources. One of the most important of these resources is a close working relationship with the contribution managers of Seattle-based companies. Mary Malarky is an assistant vice president for SAFECO Insurance Company. She serves on the advisory board, which helps direct the activities of Projection Transition.

Malarky: We are taking a very careful look at organizations that are providing very essential kind of care, almost emergency kind of care in the community that have severely cut back—health or food or shelter—something of that kind. It's kind of a life-or-death situation. We were first able to drop the criteria and then identify the agencies that had programs that we felt fit our criteria, then we approached the agencies and said, "Project Transition exists, this is what it hopes to do; here's an application and an outline proposal." And then we waited for the agencies to respond to that. It was a fairly short process and at the same time we didn't have to deal with a tremendous number of applications from agencies that weren't already delivering those services.

AO'D: Project Transition has raised $1.5 million. So far, about $1.3 million of that has been distributed to 31 agencies providing emergency services: health clinics, senior chore services, food banks, day-care facilities. According to Peter Maurer, the purpose of Project Transition is not to completely carry the load, or even to shift dependency of non-profits from government to business. It is simply to buy time so that service groups can get better organized to handle increased burdens.

Maurer: It's obviously a time for reorganizing priorities and perhaps making some very tough decisions on which agencies need to be supported. There will be some social and health service agencies that won't survive the next few years but I think the agencies that provide services that are needed in the community will certainly continue to survive and grow. Anyway, I would hope so.

AO'D: This summer the advisory board will meet again, to evaluate the project and its effect in helping fill important gaps. At that time it will be decided if Project Transition needs to be continued into 1983.

In the City of Neighborhoods, I'm Arthur O'Donnell.

Metrocenter YMCA

Jarleth Hume: The foundation people are also getting flooded, and they are turning down *en masse* all of the form proposals that people send in. If you blanket the countryside with proposals, you can't really expect to get any kind of a positive response.

AO'D: If necessity is indeed the mother of invention, non-profit groups will be coming up with many new and creative ways to cope with the 1980s. They have to, because many of the old ideas for generating revenue just don't work anymore.

Groups which relied on government funding are now turning to the private sector, but it should be obvious that in this economy, business and foundations cannot even come close to handling the increased demand. Even those groups which are most successful at tapping private sector support are finding these are difficult times.

One such group is Seattle's Metro Center YMCA. In 1973, Metro Center was set up as one of four similar groups around the country. The idea, according to director Jarleth Hume, was that government could not handle all problems, and citizens might be able to come up with better ideas.

Hume: We've always had a lot of different kinds of programs but the focus on all those programs is looking at ways that people at the local level can take initiatives to deal with their basic urban needs—housing, energy, food—those kinds of necessities.

AO'D: Seattle's Metrocenter is by far the most successful of the four programs started by the YMCA in 1973. It has overseen many grassroots media projects and weatherization programs and has helped to find funding for dozens of other groups.

Perhaps its biggest successes are an annual resource guide to non-profit organizations called the People's Yellow Pages and two different events called City Fair, stressing individual self-help and urban survival ideas.

Last year Metrocenter's budget was $1.8 million. Funds came in from 50 different sources. So far this year, it's difficult to tell how fundraising is going but Metrocenter's long experience gives it a distinct advantage in keeping up its contacts and determining what directions private giving will take.

Steve Silha used to work with the Mott Foundation, one of this nation's largest contributors to neighborhood-oriented groups. He now works for Metrocenter, keeping in touch with the foundation scene.

Silha: For the past 20 years or so, most foundations have wanted to be on the leading edge. They've wanted to fund the innovative, high-risk programs, or at least that's the way their philosophies read. But some foundations are taking a new look at their objectives and saying well maybe we should fill in the gaps.

AO'D: In 1981, foundation giving stayed steady at $2.5 billion. One reason is that endowment portfolios were unable to grow in the depressed economic climate. So what does this mean for grant seekers? According to Jarleth Hume, it means a basic redefinition of the kinds of projects to do, given available resources.

Hume: You're raising resources with those funds because there's enormous amounts of resources that are non-cash that can be put into programs that in many ways are easier to get than cash and in terms of accomplishing your objectives are just as valuable.

AO'D: Another important goal will be to conceive of projects that do several things at once, fill basic society needs *and* aim towards eventual self-sufficiency. Just recently Metrocenter began a summer employment project sponsored with downtown business. The project will help keep downtown streets and sidewalks clean, as well as give valuable job-finding experience to teenagers.

Hume: Foundation people tell me that they're going to be looking much more favorably at projects that first of all that they're needed by society, the things that everybody can agree, we need this. And second, that it's something that could become revenue-generating over a period of time and a foundation would feel good about funding something for two or three years if after that time it could find a way to generate its own income.

Silha: But there's many non-profit organizations that it would be completely inappropriate for them to try to bring in enough revenue to kind of pay their own way because they're dealing with a type of need and with a type of person that there's actually incapable of paying for. That's just a fact and that's got to be accepted.

AO'D: Jarleth Hume, Steve Silha and others at Metrocenter see a need for new ideas and creative solutions to the problems of American cities. They say that people who truly believe they've found a good idea to help people can find a source of funding if they're persistent.

Hume: Come up with a good idea, figure out how to communicate that idea in a clear, maybe different way. But simple, keep it simple. Third, don't be afraid to ask anybody for anything that you need. And then fourth, to be accountable for what it is you say you are going to do, to do a good job of evaluating and then to get back to your funding source and say, "This is what we did. We accomplished what we said we were going to do and more."

In the City of Neighborhoods, I'm Arthur O'Donnell.

Common Ground

AO'D: The Emil Hotel used to be a good example of a bad place to live. Broken windows, falling plaster and dingy walls all added to a sense of helplessness. But the Emil Hotel has been reborn. In September it was purchased by Seattle's First United Methodist Church. In six months, windows, walls, and atmosphere have all been replaced. Even the name is new. The Emil Hotel has been re-christened the Pulliam/Wesley Haven and it will serve as the home for 30 low-income and elderly residents. Throughout this transition, a non-profit group called Common Ground worked behind the scenes, helping the church with technical assistance. Steve Claggett is the director of Common Ground.

Claggett: Our dream last year was simply to get a new church to lease a residential building downtown and so we'd be assured that at least for the next ten years that housing would continue to be available. We were extremely fortunate to find the interest in First United Methodist Church to buy a low-income residential hotel.

AO'D: Common Ground's mission is to improve housing opportunities for low and fixed-income persons. It partners in this with churches and parishes in the Greater Seattle region. In the aftermath of federal and state cutbacks, churches and synagogues have seen an increased demand for what was once a major a part of their ministry, aid to the aged and poor. For Social Service groups, the religious segment of the private sector represents a virtually untapped source of financial and charitable aid. Sister Kathleen Pruitt acts as a liaison between Common Ground and the church community, helping to urge a greater social action on the part of congregations.

Pruitt: The mandate of the Gospel in effect is that the churches must be attuned to and concerned for the health and human needs of the people in the community in which they live.

AO'D: Community organizers have long recognized the potential role for churches. The followers of Saul Alinsky often use churches and parishes as a foundation for community support, resources, and money.

Pruitt: The church is a stable organization. The church plays a prominent role in the lives of many, many people, and the church is traditionally sensitive to those issues of human concern.

AO'D: The Pulliam/Wesley Haven is a perfect example of a Common Ground project. Last year the First United Methodist Church began to think about leasing and renovating an older building for use by low-income persons. Common Ground came in and showed the church that it would cheaper to buy the Emil Hotel property.

Claggett: The church voted to do that, it was by no means unanimous. It was slightly over half but the church really got behind this project. There was a fellow named Dudley Pulliam, who had been a member of this church and involved with a housing task force, was very excited about this project. He died prior to the commencement of the project so he had some money he left the church, and they used the money from his estate to purchase the Emil Hotel.

AO'D: Then Common Ground really went to work securing a $175,000 loan from Seattle block grant funds—providing a little bit of money and the technical assistance needed to carry the project through.

Claggett: We set up Common Ground to operate on a model that wherever possible Common Ground would not own and operate its own housing but would find churches and groups such as First United Methodist, that would—in the long run—own and manage. We would simply help them develop and make the project come into being.

AO'D: Now the Pulliam/Wesley Haven is ready for use by 30 residents who will pay between $75 and $125 dollars a month for furnished rooms with community restrooms and shared kitchens.

Despite the best efforts of groups like Common Ground and the First United Methodist Church, it would be unwise to expect the religious sector to completely fill the gaps left by government cuts, but Steve Claggett sees a significant role for churches in providing affordable housing for those who really need it.

Claggett: If each church has one or two housing projects, they can provide more attention to their housing, and there can be more differentiation and diversity between one project and another.

In the City of Neighborhoods, I'm Arthur O'Donnell.

Seattle Emergency Housing

AO'D: For the Seattle Emergency Housing Service, the past ten years have been ones of capacity houses and turning customers away. While a theater company might be happy with such a record, emergency shelter is another matter. The drama is real life, and every person turned away means another family without a place to sleep. Martha Diltz is the director of Seattle Emergency Housing.

Diltz: In 1980 we turned away an average of 284 families every month. Last month we turned away 472 families who requested our service, and that's an incredible increase.

AO'D: The Emergency Housing Service was begun in the aftermath of Seattle's last big recession, the Boeing Bust. At that time volunteers took it upon themselves to find a few apartments that might serve as temporary shelter for families who'd lost their homes. In the decade that followed, Seattle's economy bounced up and down, but the demand for emergency shelter stayed high.

During the boom years families served were often new to Seattle, drawn by hopes of finding employment. Others were displaced by condominium development or skyrocketing rental costs.

According to Martha Diltz, today's clients, more and more, are from the middle class. She calls them "The New Poor."

Diltz: The increase in the request for our services mainly come from people who have jobs and have secure places in the communities, who owned homes, who've been laid off and after a period of three to six months finally felt destitute. And there are no longer the resources in the community to help them put their lives back together.

AO'D: The picture remains bleak. But oddly enough, despite social service cutbacks at every level of government, Seattle's Emergency Housing Service is expanding its operation to help more people.

There are two reasons for this. One is the special emphasis by corporations on emergency services during hard times. Emergency Housing was the only United Way agency to receive an extra $20,000 share of money from Project Transition. Another reason is the service's success as an organization. In many ways, Emergency Housing is a fine example of a small but efficient non-profit agency, especially in its relationship between the staff and the board of directors.

Diltz: I think when you take a look at organizations and why private non-profits succeed or fail, it really boils down to people. We have always been very fortunate in that we were able to attract people who had a strong commitment and a strong vision of our service, available to focus most of our positive energy into the services and not into dealing with board rifts or rifts between the staff and the board.

AO'D: The board of directors for a non-profit agency has become a critical element in its economic survival. First of all, the board lends credibility to an agency. They are the people with contacts to the private sector. Sometimes with fund-raising connections to the foundations, corporations, and individual donors.

Diltz: Each one of our board know hundreds of people, and boards that are really committed and enthused about what they are doing, talk about that, you know, to other people and get our message across that what's happening to families in this community.

AO'D: Just as important, the board is a resource of special skills and information that can be valuable, planning the future, and avoiding problems.

Diltz: We have had the advantage of always having some planners on our board, two-and-a-half years before the CETA cuts, we foresaw the CETA was going to wrap up and become a thing of the past. We pretty much divorced ourselves from CETA. We always had a few CETA workers but always auxiliary programs, never core staff.

AO'D: In the case of Emergency Housing, the board of directors is continually facing the challenge of keeping the agency on track and charting new directions. The board draws from real-estate brokers and urban planners, people with accounting and budgeting skills, and those with grant-writing expertise.

Diltz: When we recruit board people, we are very clear on what kind of people we need with what kind of skills. The board goes out and actively recruits those people and then very actively orients them and includes them into the agency and finds appropriate ways for them to become active on the board.

AO'D: According to Martha Diltz, the future will find the board of Emergency Housing even more involved in the effort to reach self-sufficiency. Soon the agency would like to purchase a small apartment building for its units, rather than relying on rental units from Seattle's Housing Authority. And there is the possibility of setting up a small business to generate revenue and provide clients with useful employment during their shelter.

These bold steps require imagination and leadership from dedicated staff and board members. Seattle's Emergency Housing is lucky enough to claim both as resources.

In the City of Neighborhoods, I'm Arthur O'Donnell.

The Nature Conservancy

Elliott Marks: The most powerful argument I can make is totally solid, and that's taking someone out and showing them what we're trying to buy and saying, "Look, here it is, and you're walking on it." And it, in itself, is usually quite beautiful and has its own appeal, and you don't have to say a word. And you say, "Here it is, we need this much money to protect it. Gonna help?" And the land itself is our most powerful argument.

AO'D: Elliott Marks is a field representative for the Seattle branch of the Nature Conservancy, and he spends a lot of time in fields, and in the mountains and forests of the Northwest.

The Nature Conservancy is not the usual kind of community organization. Its membership is nationwide, some 120,000 people in all. But unlike many non-profit groups, its true constituency is not people but trees, plants, and animals. Since 1950 the Nature Conservancy has been in the business of saving land from development, and business has been very good. It is the oldest and largest land trust in the United States. Over the past 20 years its bought nearly two million acres of land. Today it still manages 700 preserves scattered in every state.

According to Elliot Marks, much of the success stems from thinking and acting like a business. He calls the Conservancy the real-estate arm of the environmental movement.

Marks: What we do fits in very well with what mainstream America believes in. We essentially answer the question of people who say, "If you think it's so important, why don't you buy it?" Well that's exactly what we do, we go out and buy it.

AO'D: As a non-profit agency the Conservancy relies upon membership dues, individual contributions and foundation grants for its money. Part of the field rep's job is to raise those funds—a job that gets harder every year.

Marks: It's very clear that fundraising is going to be more difficult this year than it was last. Needs have grown a great deal in terms of government cutbacks. The incentives of the private sector to support those needs have been significantly reduced by the tax law provisions that came into effect in 1982.

AO'D: There are many lessons that non-profit groups and business ventures could learn from the Conservancy, but a key concept is called leveraging—taking one asset and using it to generate other assets. To explore all the ways that the group uses leveraging, let's take an example of a recent Conservancy project here in the Northwest preserving the grasslands of Eastern Washington.

Marks: We found in our research that the Columbia Basin types of ecosystems were the most threatened types in the state of Washington, had received the least amount of attention and were quite fragmentary. So that if we didn't act quickly, they simply would be gone.

AO'D: To purchase these lands, the Washington Nature Conservancy has access to a pool of money from the national organization—a revolving fund, especially for use in securing options on land.

Marks: Essentially you can take the same money and recycle it over and over again and we do that constantly, to utilize fairly limited resources to get maximum result in terms of lands protected.

AO'D: When the land is secured, Marks then begins his outside fundraising, first producing a brochure to raise Conservancy members' interest in the project. Then, he seeks his first big contributor.

Marks: You're going to get 90 percent of your money from 10 percent or less of your contributors and so you put a relatively small amount of time and expense into getting the small contributions, you have your material do that for you. Then you focus your efforts and time on the people who are capable of making larger contributions that will really make or break your campaign. We talked a little bit about leverages. We went to a national foundation that had an interest in grasslands and we received a commitment from them of $150,000 as a challenge grant. It would put in one dollar for every dollar that was contributed by someone here in Washington. We had a good amount of leverage there in the sense of being able to go to people and say, "Give us ten and we'll get ten more from somebody else."

AO'D: You can see that the goal has already been cut in half from $300,000 to $150,000 through leveraging power. But leveraging does not stop there.

Marks: The foundations and corporations quite often look at each other to see what each other is doing before they will commit themselves. So if you target X-Corporation as a potential donor and they come through, then you can essentially leverage that support by going to Y and Z and saying, "X is supporting us, won't you?"

AO'D: At present, the Washington Grasslands Project is still shy of its goal, but Marks is confident of the eventual success of the project, and the continued success of the Nature Conservancy.

Marks: Because we're the only game in town. If we don't do it, land is not going to be protected, and people understand that, and people are continuing to contribute to make that possible.

In the City of Neighborhoods, I'm Arthur O'Donnell.

Neighborhood Reinvestment Corporation

AO'D: Mr. Wilson had made up his mind. He was going to stay in his South Tacoma home, fix up the outside, get a new roof, and try and make his neighborhood look a little less timeworn. Who knows? Maybe somebody else on the block will pick up the idea too. But to do a good job, it would take at least $24,000.

The bank wanted 18 percent interest and probably wouldn't even give him the whole amount. Mr. Wilson was able to get that loan—two loans in fact—one for $10,000 at 18 percent from the bank, the other for $14,000 at 5 percent from the South Tacoma Neighborhood Housing Service.

South Tacoma's NHS is one of 160 in 100 cities around the country. Most concentrate on single-family neighborhoods, but more and more they're becoming involved in multi-family and commercial projects. The Neighborhood Housing Services is a non-profit organization that represents a 3-way partnership of residents, city, and corporate participation. And each NHS has a relationship with the Neighborhood Reinvestment Corporation of Washington, D.C. Chuck Weinstock is Seattle's representative for Neighborhood Reinvestment.

Weinstock: Neighborhood Reinvestment, at the request of a local government or lenders or a neighborhood group, comes in as a sort of neutral entity and develops the program. Once it's incorporated, we have no legal relationship. They're not subsidiaries. They're all private, locally controlled groups. I think that's part of the beauty.

AO'D: The staff of a local NHS receives training from Neighborhood Reinvestment in every phase needed for systematic community revitalization—from grassroots canvassing to sophisticated financial negotiations. Art Gordon is the director for South Tacoma's NHS.

Gordon: They assisted us and they led us to a lot of the resources that we didn't know were available. They also provide some technical assistance along the way. You know, some basic how-to's.

AO'D: While most housing programs suffered severe cutbacks in the 1982 federal budget, Neighborhood Reinvestment actually saw its budget increase by 14 percent. These federal dollars formed a basis of a revolving loan fund, a pool of money that local groups can draw upon to start their projects.

Weinstock: I can say that over the past 24 months we have directly ourselves provided 22 loans, an additional 22 referring to lending institutions for loans and helping with the work write up, the specifications, contractors and things of that nature. So there's 44 loans that the NHS Program is directly involved with. The dollar amount is somewhere in the neighborhood of $500,000.

AO'D: The revolving loan idea is a well-used concept for nationwide non-profit groups and it works well, until the group finds out that all of its money is committed to projects. So Neighborhood Reinvestment took that idea one step further. In an agreement with the Aetna Life Insurance Company, Neighborhood Reinvestment has created a secondary market for the loans arranged by the NHS.

Weinstock: NHS, when they have made loans and when those loans are current, can sell those loans on the secondary market and re-capitalize their revolving loan fund. They're able to sell up to half of their portfolio. So they get $300,000 from the city, say, in a couple years that's all lent out. They can sell a hundred and fifty of that.

AO'D: Chuck Weinstock says the use of a secondary market by non-profit housing groups is unique to the NHS system and it's proving a valuable tool for getting needed dollars directed back into the neighborhoods.

Gordon: It's a way to marshal funds so that that scarce pool of money goes as far as possible.

AO'D: Another goal of the Neighborhood Housing Service is to continually adjust to changing situations, to develop new tools and techniques for preserving neighborhoods for the benefit of current residents.

Gordon: In addition, it's making money go farther. One of the basic goals is to increase private investment in the neighborhood as much as residents think it's necessary so that the NHS can do its job, stabilize the neighborhood and get out—treat the neighborhood—and then it will take care of itself.

AO'D: Neighborhood Reinvestment Corporation and the Neighborhood Housing Service model is an outstanding example of a community-oriented non-profit meeting the challenges of the 1980s. Success can be measured in a number of ways in the number of homes renovated in a new spirit of public and private cooperation and in maintaining resident control over the development of their neighborhood.

Weinstock: The Neighborhood Housing Services model, bringing in the corporate sector, the city and residents really brings to bear all the influence and all the resources that you have to have to really deal with a neighborhood's problem.

Gordon: These entities now are beginning to see that it is working, and it deals with housing very well because it can do it at a much faster rate than the more traditional government-type programs could have.

In the City of Neighborhoods, I'm Arthur O'Donnell.

Randolph Carter Industrial Workshop

Marilyn Chase: Our success, I think, is seeing the person go from a dependent situation to a situation of self-sufficiency. We're achieving success when our people come and complain that they've lost their other supplemental support because they're making too much money.

AO'D: Marilyn Chase is an assistant director of the Randolph Carter Industrial Workshop. Since 1968, the Workshop has been serving handicapped and disturbed persons with counseling and job placement. In its efforts to make its clients economically self-sufficient, an interesting thing happened to the Workshop—it began thinking and acting like a small business, and it became 92 percent self-sufficient.

Chase: We do get about 8 percent of our budget, our cash flow, from United Way, but that's the only grant, and the rest of the money comes from our own efforts. For example, we do a lot of bench work, assembly work, landscaping—which is really a grounds keeping—lawn mowing, leaf raking. We do janitorial work. Our idea is to *create* jobs.

AO'D: These days many non-profit service groups are feeling the pinch of government cutbacks and the increase in competition for foundation support. Some are trying to develop businesses as a way of generating new revenues. According to Marilyn Chase, the Industrial Workshop found itself involved in business development as a direct outgrowth of its service to clients, many of whom were having trouble keeping jobs in which they were placed.

Chase: Across the nation about 50 percent of the developmentally disabled people who are placed in competitive employment, *do* lose their job within two months, primarily because they have never had the experience of being fired, they have never had to experience the competitiveness in a workstation discipline that they encounter in the industrial world. So we try to duplicate those conditions, and we're quite successful at it.

AO'D: Marilyn Chase says the Workshop wins contracts from companies to do small-scale industrial and maintenance work, not out of charity, but because it has a proven track record of cost-effectiveness and productivity.

Chase: Because our program tries to duplicate the conditions of competitive employment, our people know that when they can get a job, they are not being baby-sat, you know. People here work, and they feel good about it.

AO'D: Chase thinks that the Workshop's success can and should be duplicated by other agencies for the disabled, and she'd like to see Workshop programs expanded to dispel the notion that so-called "unemployables" and the agencies that help them must be forever dependent on government handouts.

Chase: If we can integrate ourselves into the broader economy and provide jobs and a defensible product, we will be in much better shape for survival than if we were dependent upon grants or philanthropic procurement for example. Our goal is to be self-sufficient as an agency and have every single person here in our program—all of our participants—as self-sufficient individuals.

In the City of Neighborhoods, I'm Arthur O'Donnell.

Community Health Clinics

sfx: telephone rings

Recorded voice: Hello. This is Apple-a-Day Health Information and Self-Care Center. We would like to be answering you in person, but are unable to.

AO'D: As the recorded message reveals, the Apple-a-Day Health Service is struggling for staff and survival. Because it provides preventative health services rather than remedial care, Apple-a-Day is finding itself unable to compete for the shrinking amount of dollars available to emergency health services. But there is one hope for keeping Apple-a-Day's doors open. The clinic is a member of the North Seattle Health Care Consortium. Nancy Long sits on the Consortium's board of directors.

Long: We need for the agencies to coalesce, because the funding sources simply don't want to deal with hundreds and hundreds of requests every month from every little agency out in the fertile fields of the neighborhoods.

AO'D: The funding squeeze has caused non-profit organizations around the country to look at the value of the consortium approach, but Seattle has a well-established history of consortia in health care.

Jack Thompson is administrator of the Neighborhood Health Centers of Seattle. This is a combination of eight health and dental clinics located in Seattle's low-income communities. The Consortium has been in effect since 1972.

Thompson: Individual clinics began to realize that number one, if they worked together, they could pool some of the administrative activities that went on and that meant more resources were going to be available for patient care. Two, by coordinating fund-seeking activities, they could approach things cooperatively rather than competitively, and three, I think by doing that they looked much stronger to the funding sources.

AO'D: Thompson adds that consortia do not involve a complete merger of clinics. Each of the Seattle-area 22 community clinics values its independence and separate identity. They provide health care to over 50,000 individuals, many of whom would be unable to pay for regular health care.

Thompson: That's not a population that some of the other facilities that are being built around town are real anxious to serve, because obviously there's not a lot of economic incentive to serve them.

AO'D: Another active consortium of clinics is the Central Seattle Community Health Center. This offers a different kind of umbrella for its members. Since 1976, it's concentrated on providing services and fund-raising management to five clinics. Bill Hobson is director of this consortium.

Hobson: We, for instance, have established a pharmacy and have hired a staff pharmacist for that central pharmacy. We then use that pharmacist to work with four of the five clinics in our system. We have hired a consortium nutritionist who works with four of our five clinics in support of the nutrition education programs that we have of each of our clinics.

AO'D: Even with these three consortia in effect, Seattle's community clinics are facing rough times. Funding cuts are not new, and the rise of unemployment has added a new burden on services—thousands of new patients whose regular health benefits have ended with their jobs.

Hobson: We have taken a number of cuts over five years and now we're getting to the point that the cuts are starting to occur in the basic sources of support that are left.

Long: How much can we pretend to do? You cannot do adequate high-quality health care through totally volunteer, piecemeal, put-together programs. You need ongoing programs with ongoing stable staff; you need ongoing funding to provide that.

AO'D: In response to the challenge, Seattle's health care system is currently looking at new ideas for improving efficiency, and for keeping its services available to thousands who depend upon them.

It's been suggested that two of the three consortia might consider a merger, if all of the individual clinics can see a benefit. At any rate, Jack Thompson feels the consortium approach gives clinics a head start on developing new survival strategies.

Thompson: In proving our efficiency, we're prioritizing what services we're going to be providing, toward increasingly sharing resources, although, you know, I think the strength of the consortium approach is that we have the ability to do that. We're already set up to try to share resources, to share staff, to prioritize what services we're going to provide to the different communities, to do a lot of problem-solving among the clinics in some kind of a forum.

In the City of Neighborhoods, I'm Arthur O'Donnell.

Section Two: It's My Backyard, Too

NIMBY and Energy 1990–2001

NIMBY—A Reporter's Perspective

THE VERY FIRST TIME I encountered the Not In My Back Yard (NIMBY) syndrome was in 1975 in Eugene, Oregon. Employed as a fry cook in a not-so-fast food restaurant on the midnight-to-six shift, I spent my days trying to break into radio (KZEL-FM, album-oriented rock) as a local news reporter with an attitude. Aside from covering city council meetings and taping occasional interviews with visiting celebrities, I worked the neighborhood news beat documenting the activities of community groups in that small but politically vibrant college town.

My first real story was about the proposed construction of a Bi-Mart supermarket and department store—a forerunner to the Costco discount warehouse—in a residential neighborhood. I remember the developer as a classic villain who tried to build his store without benefit of a zoning variance; he was the kind of business owner who would glad-hand politicians with promises of jobs for the economically depressed community but then bring in a non-union construction crew from out-of-state.

He did not let me tape record an interview but smiled all the while through our discussion, denying any knowledge of community concerns about noise, heavy traffic flow or parking problems associated with his development. That was at 1 p.m. I soon found out from local sources that the Bi-Mart man had previously arranged a 2 p.m. meeting that same day with the neighborhood group to tell them he would fight at every turn their attempts to negotiate mitigations. Despite my impassioned denunciations of his duplicity—broadcast live at 2:45—the store was eventually built.

Five years later I was again doing neighborhood news, this time in Seattle for a daily public affairs feature carried by a half-dozen radio stations. In the corridors of City Hall, I can recall interviewing a woman neighborhood activist who had just delivered an impassioned speech against municipal efforts to locate a low-income housing project on her street.

The same issues—parking, traffic flow and preservation of neighborhood character—were what she raised against the project. By then I was sophisticated enough to recognize the real meaning of her code words; she wanted to prevent poor blacks from moving onto her block. In that instance, the neighborhood opposition was successful; the housing project was forced to locate elsewhere.

Both of these stories from the past are examples of NIMBY. I've encountered many others over the years but these two stand out in my memory, perhaps because of their perverse outcomes—at least to my perspective. On one hand, an honest effort by neighbors trying to maintain the integrity of their residential community was defeated by overriding commercial considerations. On the other, what I interpreted as a selfish attempt to scuttle a needed low-income housing project was successful because of political pressure adroitly applied by an ad-hoc obstructionist organization.

I resurrect these two tales as a kind of preface for what I intend to be a series of columns on NIMBY activism directed against power project construction here in California and in other parts of the West. Even with the current emphasis on energy efficiency as a way to displace prospective generating projects, there inevitably will be a need for "green field development" of new resources. And even with the competitive field tilted toward what might otherwise be considered politically correct renewable resources or natural gas-fired cogeneration, the market will witness continuing battles between well-financed developers and well-organized community activists who would rather see the proposed facilities sited in somebody else's—anybody else's—backyard.

Certainly, no particular resource is immune to NIMBY opposition. A proposed wind farm near smog-bound Los Angeles was killed by neighborhood concerns over potential noise, visual impacts and supposed threats to the protected California Condor. The Crockett cogeneration plant went into developmental hiatus largely because of community opposition to the way it intended to store ammonia for its air emission reduction technology. About the same time, well-heeled neighborhoods north of San Diego managed to scuttle a proposed waste-to-energy project at the San Marcos landfill.

Not long ago, I visited the Puna geothermal project in Hawaii, which was unable to commence operations because of guerrilla warfare conducted by a small but sophisticated group of local residents. Those activists would rather live with power blackouts on a hopelessly overloaded utility system than allow commercial development of the geothermal resource along the slopes of the Kilauea volcano.

In each of these instances, environmental arguments voiced by concerned NIMBYites played a crucial role in the fight against development. I was struck, for instance, by the irony apparent in Hawaii. The people who slapped "Unplug Geothermal Power" bumper stickers on their cars in Puna appeared to be the same kinds of folks in my San Francisco neighborhood whose cars sport "Support Renewable Energy" signs.

Much has been written about the linkage of environmentalism and NIMBY activism, and many observers have reached the conclusion that while NIMBY opponents of a particular project may mouth environmental arguments, they do not truly accept broader environmental ethics. Their real concern is often the preservation of property rights and their own property values; but like the Seattle woman who opposed public housing in her neighborhood, NIMBY opponents will voice whatever arguments they can to attain credibility. And while they consistently portray themselves as underdogs in a fight against some big, bad developer, NIMBYites are able to recruit some very powerful allies—notably established environmental groups and members of the media who will always give time to covering "David vs. Goliath" stories—when they begin to espouse environmental arguments against their opponents.

Bob Kahn, a public relations consultant for some wind and biomass development clients, once sent me a copy of an address he gave to Washington State legislators that touched upon this linkage of NIMBY and environmental activism. "By their very participation," Kahn said, "environmentalist support expands the opposition's rationale and takes it to a 'higher' plane. A green-tinted NIMBY opposition is more powerful because it moves the argument beyond narrow self-interest."

Nearly 20 years have passed since I started my professional reporting career, but I will admit that I now feel less able to judge the legitimacy of opposition to proposed developments. That is one difficulty of being trained to honor all sides of contentious issues. But the task remains: How to discover what really separates a self-serving NIMBY activist from a true environmentalist, and what a worthy project needs to do to overcome NIMBY opposition.

[August 1992]

How GWF Won Over the City of Hanford

EVERY NEW DEVELOPMENT HAS OPPONENTS. Sometimes the adversaries are few but so dedicated and so tenacious that the project is put into legal or economic jeopardy—or even killed off completely. Victory is often the result of a long recruitment campaign tapping disparate community members who have a special interest in maintaining the status quo or blocking development.

The most powerful and successful coalitions are those that include a broader community than those who simply cry "Not In My Back Yard!" when change threatens their property. When NIMBYites enlist the sympathy and support of recognized groups—especially environmental and media organizations—they have a much greater chance of stopping or detouring development. And if that coalition manages to swing public opinion to its side, a developer can do little but pack up and move on.

Or so it would seem. But at least one developer of an unpopular power project continued to hang on despite unbeatable odds to win over even its most adamant opponents and bring its plant into commercial operation. The developer is GWF Power Systems and the project is a 27 MW cogeneration plant in the city of Hanford in Fresno County. The case represents one of the most remarkable environmental fights in California in recent years and certainly the most amazing turnaround of NIMBY attitudes I've encountered.

The Hanford project was conceived as a showcase for an innovative technology—circulating fluidized-bed combustion (CFB), which burns fuel more efficiently and with fewer emissions than any standard combustion device. Unfortunately for GWF, the fuel was coal.

In recent years, residents of Hanford (population about 20,000) had become increasingly concerned about the impacts of rapid growth on their primarily agricultural community. In the dry bowl of the San Joaquin Valley, air pollution from the Interstate 5/Highway 99 corridor and from the smoggy Los Angeles basin had become a permanent fixture. Fresno County was cited in 1979 by the federal EPA as a non-attainment area for ozone, particulate matter and carbon monoxide.

Although much of the smog was directly attributable to auto exhaust, residents were wary of any new industrial source of pollution and were especially opposed to any potential coal burning in the region.

Opposition to the plant came from two community groups, the Kings County Farm Bureau and the Citizens for a Healthy Environment, which relied on environmental arguments against the city granting permits. The Farm Bureau blamed air pollution for reduced crop yields and economic losses of hundreds of millions of dollars. Any claims of environmental benefits or job creations from GWF's plant were drowned out by the steady cry "No-to-Coal." The groups added legal muscle to the fight by hiring an activist law firm that was also spearheading the successful effort to close Sacramento's Rancho Seco nuclear project.

The entire community was involved in the controversy. Public opinion surveys showed that nearly 95 percent of the population knew about GWF's plans to build the plant and 80 percent expressed some level of opposition to the facility, primarily because of pollution fears. In addition, GWF had little credibility and was mistrusted by residents. When a local newspaper revealed that the female mayor had an affair with GWF's project manager, the developer's image in the community tarnished further.

The political history of the Hanford project is almost too complicated to outline here, but by 1990 it created a dire situation for GWF. Although the developer initially won environmental permits from the city in March 1988, the NIMBY opponents successfully mounted a recall drive against Hanford's mayor and the council members who had supported the project. A new council elected on the No-to-Coal platform quickly proposed a ban on coal burning in the community and was joined by neighboring Fresno County, where GWF was planning a similar coal-fired project.

That's when the lawsuits began in earnest. GWF sued the city over the moratorium and eventually reached a settlement that allowed continued construction. The Farm Bureau and the Citizens went to Kings County Superior Court where they lost a challenge to the permits, then to the California Court of Appeal, which not only overturned the city permits but also declared the entire Hanford zoning code legally invalid because of its failure to consider the cumulative effects of pollution from several new sources, including the project.

The judge, however, allowed the nearly completed project to continue testing its equipment to develop a record of actual emissions for use when GWF reapplied for a city permit under a revised zoning plan. This ruling proved crucial to GWF's attempt to win back the community.

The developer finally turned to a professional community relations firm, Barnes Clarke of San Francisco, to devise and carry out a strategy for overcoming the community's opposition. The firm's goal was to change enough people's minds to pressure the activists to sit down with GWF and negotiate.

Time was short: the $70 million plant needed to begin commercial production before its operational deadline with PG&E expired, its power sales contract was voided and all was lost. The situation is best summed up by a letter to the Hanford Sentinel written by members of the Farm Bureau. "The people have said 'No-to-Coal,' the courts have said 'No-to-Coal,' and our city council has said 'No-to-Coal.' GWF does not fit here!"

New community surveys essentially reflected previous levels of opposition to coal, so Barnes Clarke and GWF embarked on a two-fold strategy to improve the developer's image in the community—by "proving" the company's claims that its technology would produce needed power with a minimum of harmful pollution and by portraying GWF as a successful, nationally recognized industry leader with positive experience in other communities.

Important elements of the "good corporate neighbor" policy included establishing a local hiring program for city residents and a targeted community donation program. To prevent being perceived as trying to buy its way into the community, GWF chose instead to fund small-scale environmental projects, such as a tree planting ceremony and a high school environmental scholarship. Its largest donation was a $60,000 grant to fund a San Joaquin Valley pollution study that measured the causes of smog in the region.

GWF president Leonard Wohadlo was brought before the national media, not to discuss the Hanford situation but to highlight GWF's five power plants in Contra Costa County that showcased pollution control and efficient burning of solid waste fuels. Each new piece of positive press was forwarded to local politicians and activists with the intent to soften their stance against the company.

Perhaps the most important strategy was an effort to get local residents to visit the Hanford project and see for themselves what the technology entailed. The consultant pursued a concerted effort to reach the community, eventually getting more than 1,400 residents to visit the plant. Individuals who reacted positively were enlisted to draw in other support, which was employed in letter-writing campaigns.

The groundwork paid off. In January 1991, GWF and its legal team from the firm Morrison & Foerster entered negotiations with the Farm Bureau and the

Citizens group that eventually reached a successful settlement. The compromise that enabled both sides to claim a victory involved a switch in the Hanford plant's fuel source, from coal to a combination of petroleum coke and natural gas. The opposition could say it prevented the coal project and GWF was able to start commercial operations and save the plant.

One measure of the amazing turnaround in opposition to the project came in the comments made by environmental representatives who signed the agreement. "The settlement demonstrates that new industries can accommodate the environmental concerns and values of local communities," said Alene Talor, president of Citizens for a Healthy Environment. "I think that this plant is now a net benefit to the area," added Jim Verhoon of the Farm Bureau.

[September 1992]

The Ballad of Crockett:
A Company Town Rebels

CROCKETT IS ONE OF THOSE PLACES YOU ARE LIKELY TO PASS BY. Carved into the bluffs along the Carquinez Strait, Crockett is the town you almost notice as you drive along Interstate 80 in Contra Costa County. For most of its history, the town has been associated most closely with two major landmarks, the C&H sugar refinery and the nearby Carquinez Bridge.

The refinery was there from the start; in fact, the plant and its smokestack can be seen on the county seal. For over 80 years Crockett was a company town. Then one day in 1984 some residents of Crockett decided they didn't want to live in a company town anymore and rebelled against C&H's plans to become a steam host for a 240 MW cogeneration plant on refinery property.

Eight years later, the plant remains unbuilt and the controversy over the Crockett Cogeneration plant stands as one of California's major NIMBY battles of the last decade. It also indicates how, at that particular time, state policies encouraging independent cogeneration development began to unravel.

The Crockett rebellion offers a prime example of how a dedicated and highly sophisticated group of citizens can bring a sure-fire deal to a grinding halt. Whether the activists—in the form of the Crockett Improvement Association and the Crockett Power Plant Committee—represented the majority of residents or just a very loud minority was never clear, but at every public hearing on the project, the committees routinely turned out hundreds of neighbors to voice their opposition.

Some wanted to kill the project completely, others wanted to see it considerably reduced in size; some were concerned with preserving the character of the small community, others just wanted to keep their view unobstructed or maintain their property values. As the battle continued, the major arguments against the project shifted; each time the developer made a concession or seemed to gain a political or regulatory victory, the opposition would come back again with new arguments and new reasons to halt construction.

Unlike the activists who fought the Hanford coal plant, Crockett's NIMBY-ites never resorted to court action against the developer, Pacific Thermonetics Incorporated (PTI). Instead, they formed a presence at every permitting agency and regulatory board the project had to face, until a stalemate was reached at the California Energy Commission in 1989. Three years later, the Crockett plant proposal is again up for CEC consideration.

The original developer, PTI, has since been replaced by Energy National (a.k.a. Pacific Generation), the development affiliate of utility PacifiCorp, which was a more silent partner at the beginning. The original plans for the project have changed; even the plant's power sales arrangement with PG&E was significantly altered in the interim. Most of the opposition has been won over and much of the controversy quelled, but members of the Power Plant Committee still hound the siting process and testify against the need for the plant. Whichever side wins the fight will be able to claim the unofficial title of "most stubborn contender in a NIMBY encounter."

That the outcome should be determined at the CEC is fitting, because the community first found out about the project from the commission—although somewhat indirectly.

In the summer of 1984, Crockett resident Mary Moutinho was chatting on the telephone with a friend who worked at the commission. "What do you think about the power plant going up across the street from you?" the friend asked Moutinho, who expressed surprise. "Oh, you didn't know?"

The developer, who held a standard offer power sales agreement with Pacific Gas & Electric, previously filed for certification of the plant from the CEC, but its application was rejected for lack of information. By the time PTI was ready to resubmit its application, everyone in Crockett knew about it.

The first local public gathering to discuss the Crockett plant was sponsored by the Crockett Chamber of Commerce on September 19, 1984, drawing 500 residents into the auditorium of the local high school. Since the unincorporated town of 3,000 persons did not even have an elected mayor or city council, the chamber decided it had a responsibility to assess the situation. The event was supposed to be an informational presentation by PTI, but it quickly became a debate over the need for the project.

Most vocal were residents of Loring Avenue, whose houses were located as close as 40 feet from the plant site. Their complaints included potential noise, visual impacts and fears that the plant would create harmful air pollution. Speakers alluded to the Crockett area as a "cancer belt" because of a recorded cluster of lung cancers many times higher than average.

The reaction against the plant included another common NIMBY theme as well, that of opposition to an outside entity. Although the C&H plant was a well-respected institution, many people in Crockett objected to the Oklahoma City-based PTI because they perceived the firm as being solely interested in the profits and tax benefits the cogeneration plant could accrue. As one resident put it, "We don't want a bunch of J.R. Ewing types coming in here."

The project also conflicted with a growing movement within the community to change the town's image from an industrial site to a more tourism-oriented town. Some residents harbored a vision of Crockett as another Sausalito because of its waterfront location. A major industrial development simply did not fit their perception of the town's future.

Persons who were especially vocal at the first meeting formed the core of opposition to the Crockett plant, naming themselves the Power Plant Committee. Within days of the chamber of commerce meeting, the Crockett Improvement Association's board unanimously voted to oppose the project. Members of the groups began to educate themselves about the proposal, scrutinizing every aspect of the original CEC certification file to prepare for PTI's refiling, which came in December.

By that time, energy commission officials were highly aware of the controversy. CEC chair Charles Imbrecht said he was "impressed by the sophistication and seriousness" of the activists, and ordered agency staff and PTI to respond to the citizens' list of application deficiencies before the commission would accept the filing.

In March 1985 the CEC deemed the application "data adequate" and voted to begin the year-long review process, but more controversy followed when commissioner Arturo Gandara asked to be replaced as presiding member of the certification review committee. Gandara told the West County Times he felt the commission was "wrong" to accept the application. Instead, commissioner Warren Noteware was named to the committee. At the CEC's first public hearing on the application, about 250 persons—many wearing "plantbusters" T-shirts—loudly questioned whether the project would provide any real benefits to the community. The message they left with PTI and C&H officials was, "Gentlemen, go somewhere else. We don't want you."

By this time, Pacific Thermonetics recognized it had a very tough fight on its hands and hired the public relations firms of Sway & Company and Robert D. Kahn & Company to try to win the community to its side.

Second Impressions About Crockett Cogeneration

"You never get a second chance to make a first impression." This public relations axiom seems especially apt when discussing the Crockett Cogeneration project, because the original developer, Pacific Thermonetics Company (PTI), was never able to recover from the poor first impression it left with the Crockett community.

The town found out about the plant in 1984 through an "inadvertent news release," a chance telephone conversation between a local resident and a state employee who knew about the proposal. Soon the whole town was buzzing with news of the project and PTI lost its best chance to present the plan in a favorable light. Even though the project promised to improve the competitive posture of Crockett's largest and oldest business citizen, the C&H Sugar refinery, there was a strong and growing sentiment that the development would be destructive to the town.

Two opposition groups, the Crockett Improvement Association and the Crockett Power Plant Committee, claimed support from hundreds of residents and showed their organizational muscle at public hearings before the Contra Costa County Board of Supervisors and the California Energy Commission.

"Everything was really going to hell," recalled Bob Kahn, a public relations consultant contracted by PTI in 1985 to help win support for the cogen plant. "Our charge was to keep things from getting worse, to contain the damage and buy time."

The first task was to make sure the county supervisors did not vote to oppose the plant, even though there was "every indication" they might. Kahn worked closely with another consultant, Brian Sway of Sway & Company, who was hired to conduct permitting for PTI.

In an unusual first step, the consultants found themselves agreeing with part of the community's argument against the plant—that the proposed location along Loring Avenue, close to the homes of the most vocal opponents, was unacceptable and must be changed. The slogan they came up with, "Good plant, bad location," became a kind of mantra repeated in every contact with politicians, bureaucrats and even the project engineers, who eventually relented and agreed to relocate the unit away from the street and behind a row of sugar storage bins deeper inside C&H's property boundaries.

Although this key response enabled PTI to win firm support from the supervisors, it really made no difference to leaders of the residential opposition, who simply began to emphasize other arguments against the plant, such as the noise or visual impact it would create. Kahn described the process of negotiating with community members and permitting agencies as a "mitigation spiral" in which every concession meant to solve a problem led to another problem requiring mitigation.

When people complained about overhead transmission lines connecting the plant to Pacific Gas & Electric's system, PTI agreed to run the lines underground. But that strategy caused a problem where the lines crossed a wildlife habitat, so the route had to be changed again.

When the community raised pollution concerns before the air quality district, PTI was required to install expensive selective catalytic reduction (SCR) equipment to reduce nitrogen oxide (NOx) levels well below legal standards. But since SCR requires ammonia for injection, PTI would have to store the chemical on site, raising a fear among residents that an accident could release toxic fumes throughout the town. PTI learned it couldn't ignore these problems, but it couldn't completely solve them either (in fact, the ammonia storage concern would later become a crucial consideration). The many changes added millions to the total cost of development.

Although first impressions indicated the town was solidly against the project, Kahn said closer investigation revealed a split in the community that could be managed to PTI's benefit.

He found a solid base of support for the project—and C&H's need for the plant—among the town's older, predominantly Italian-American residents. By and large, the project also received support from the established political power base in the county: the supervisors, local newspaper publishers, chamber of commerce and citizens groups who represented old-time Crockett residents.

"Eventually," Kahn said, "we matched the opposition man for man, letter [to the editor] for letter, petition drive for petition drive. They filled the halls, we filled the halls, matching body for body at a minimum. But at that stage it was not enough. We demonstrated a countervailing force, but unless you can overwhelm the opposition, you can't win. The best we could do is what we did."

PTI's struggle for acceptance of the project was especially acute at the California Energy Commission, where staff members were beginning to question the wisdom of allowing large numbers of new gas-fired power plants to reach operation in a short period of time. Because of federal law and the state's policy encouraging independent power production, utilities were required to sign power purchase contracts with hundreds of entrepreneurial ventures. The flood of applicants for lucrative standard-offer contracts was so great that people began alluding to a modern California "gold rush."

By the time PTI was trying to move its certification application through the CEC, the state's other regulatory body, the CPUC, suspended availability of new QF contracts, and PG&E was engaging in anti-cogeneration strategies.

The CEC, responding to the perceived glut of new capacity, was formulating new rules governing its determinations on whether a power plant was "needed" on economic, physical and environmental grounds. In a major blow to PTI, the CEC determined that Crockett would have to undergo its review according to the more stringent rules of the 1985 Electricity Report (ER 5), allowing residential opponents and CEC staff to question the project's size and economic justification.

Attorneys and consultants who worked on the case for PTI recalled their frustration with the situation; they felt CEC staff was changing the siting rules as they went along, and they believed staff had taken on the cause of the project's opponents, giving credence to all sorts of arguments the developer thought it answered in other forums and demanding new concessions from the plant.

Also, because nearly all the public hearings were held in Crockett, a large contingent of opponents was always on hand. Brian Sway called it "abuse of the system," although former CEC personnel do not recall it the same way. One, a former hearing officer on the case, said he felt the CEC process was more objective in determining the need for the plant than it would have been if it were conducted by a local board or council that could be influenced by political considerations.

Political or not, it was clear that the CEC was developing its own agenda regarding cogeneration that put it at odds with CPUC policies encouraging development. And PTI was caught in the middle. One argument that seemed to find a sympathetic ear with CEC staff was that the project was far too large; the community and the utility did not need the full 240 MW of capacity offered by the plant.

In a staff analysis issued in April 1986—after a full year of hearings—CEC staff called for denying PTI's application, citing "irretrievable environmental harm" and project size as reasons for rejection. The CEC siting committee soon followed with its own recommendation to reject the project.

Faced with the very real possibility that it would lose the entire deal, PTI hired more heavyweight consultants, including William Bagley, who had recently left his position as a commissioner on the CPUC. Bagley's job was to salvage the project as best he could, and he began by contacting CEC commissioners and talking with the utility about contract changes that might make Crockett more acceptable to regulators. The actions led to an outcry from plant opponents that PTI was improperly lobbying commission decisionmakers.

Soon the developer announced a new arrangement with PG&E, negotiated by Bagley, that altered the project's operations from base-load to completely dispatchable by the utility. PTI asked the CEC to reopen the case record to accept the contract changes as revised evidence of need for the plant. This the commission did, leading to another two years of delay and additional hearings on every aspect of the plant.

PTI knew it would not be able to build the project in time to meet its PG&E contract deadline, which initially specified an August 1989 start date. Instead it again renegotiated the pact, receiving a unique settlement; PG&E agreed to pay the plant $17 million to defer operation by at least five years. PG&E stated it felt the arrangement would prevent an expensive lawsuit by PTI, but the terms of the agreement caused considerable controversy. The CPUC voted to slash the deferral payment to $12.7 million if the project reached operation by 1994.

To members of the Crockett community opposing the plant, the deferral agreement was "a colossal rip-off" that further stiffened their resolve. "I'd say there is no compromise with us unless they come in with a 25 or 30 MW plant," said Douglas Tubbs, head of the Crockett Power Plant Committee.

But in the end PTI could compromise no further. Despite everything the company did to mitigate neighborhood complaints and regulatory concerns, the CEC siting committee concluded that the plant was not needed and that the ammonia storage plan endangered the community. With that recommendation before the CEC, the developer finally gave up, deciding in June 1989 to withdraw its certificate application from the commission, ending five years of futile struggle for PTI.

Although that would seem to be the end of the story, it is not. In fact, the Crockett project is alive and well. How could that possibly have happened?

A Celebration in Crockett

By 6 pm there was hardly a parking space left on Pomona Avenue and the party was already in full swing in the Crockett Community Center. The grey-haired fellow standing at the door smiled at everyone as he handed out small blue tickets for complimentary drinks, greeting even those few he didn't recognize as a neighbor. "Lots of room inside," he welcomed, but the tables were already filling and long lines formed at the buffet tables and bar. The chatter of neighborly talk and laughter easily drowned out the light music played by a three-piece combo on the stage.

The occasion could have been a small-town church social, a Boy Scouts awards ceremony or an evening wedding reception. Instead, the printed program that came with the free-drink tickets called it a "Community Celebration" for the Crockett Cogeneration Project. The same cogeneration plant that for nearly a decade caused division and spirited NIMBY opposition somehow brought the Crockett community together for a very special event.

Earlier in the day, dark-suited businessmen and politicians posed for photographs around a small plot of overturned dirt in a parking lot in the shadows of huge, aged storage bins at the C&H Sugar refinery, just below Loring Avenue. They held gold-painted shovels purchased at the local hardware store and talked about how the $278 million power plant would add 300 construction jobs and a few dozen permanent positions to the hard-pressed local economy.

Someone read a message from the governor, praising the new project as "an example of the type of cooperative spirit which industry, the public and government would do well to emulate in future years." Others hopefully predicted the project would be the initial step of a comprehensive "Crockett regeneration" effort made possible by the tax and community fund moneys generated by the plant.

Notably, the groundbreaking did not take place where the cogeneration plant will be built, but where it was originally intended. One of the major concessions made by project developers was to move the plant away from Loring Avenue homes to the far side of the sugar bins. The place where spade met earth marks the southern end of a pedestrian bridge that will span the Southern Pacific Railroad tracks down to the plant site and to a new public fishing pier along the shore of the Carquinez Strait.

John Miller, vice president of Energy National—the developer and half-owner of the 240 MW plant—stood off to the side, talking with Jay Gunkelman, president of the Crockett Improvement Association. Gunkelman was one of the early vocal opponents of the project, but like many other citizens, he had obviously come around to supporting the plant.

Asked what caused this remarkable turnaround, Gunkelman spoke with unstinting praise for Miller and Energy National, for their willingness to finally listen to the community's concerns and make major changes to the original design that would minimize polluting emissions, ensure safety in the handling of chemicals, and reduce visual impacts of the plant. "This is going to be the very best plant that could possibly be built," Gunkelman said, contrasting the final design to the original that caused so much concern. His comments echoed a sentiment spoken by many when describing the new cogeneration plant. "It's really a completely different project."

Miller seemed uncomfortable talking at the groundbreaking site, anxious to get over to the Community Center to make sure preparations were proceeding smoothly. Once people began arriving he calmed down considerably, circulating among the tables to greet familiar faces and thank everyone for coming out. He withstood backslapping from the politicians who crowded the end of the bar and gentle ribbing from Crockett residents who—after hundreds of hours of meetings and intense negotiations—finally came to accept Miller and the project as their own.

He even withstood a few questions from this reporter, who was most interested in identifying the critical turning points that revived a moribund project—twice rejected by energy regulators and roundly condemned as an unnecessary intrusion into a closely-knit community.

He said the big change came after Energy National took control of the project from its original partner Pacific Thermonetics, Incorporated. Charitably, he did not dwell on PTI's poor initial handling of the development, which essentially bypassed the community. When he came into the project, Miller explained, the most important task was to "discover and respond to the community's concerns in the best way we could." That process involved dozens of meetings with community members and government officials.

The primary concerns were about public safety. PTI's design was changed several times to reduce pollution and visual impacts. But the emissions control technology grafted onto the plant required ammonia storage and handling, and raised even greater worries. Crockett is, after all, just up the road from Richmond, where caustic chemical releases are unfortunately recurring events.

Even before returning to the California Energy Commission for siting approval, Energy National conducted a "world class" risk assessment of the ammonia storage situation, and made several changes to minimize the risks, Miller said. Other changes involved undergrounding and changing the route of transmission lines to avoid nearby wildlife and waterfowl habitats.

After public safety concerns were dealt with, Miller said, the next task was to ensure that Crockett residents would actually realize financial benefits from the project. Though the project would pay more than $2 million in property taxes annually, the town was not going to see any of that money because it is not an incorporated part of Contra Costa County. "We worked out a deal so that Crockett would benefit as if it were incorporated," Miller said. The county agreed to devote $400,000 per year of the tax collections to Crockett while Energy National and its partners will contribute an additional $250,000 annually.

Numerous other economic benefits were negotiated by the town: assurances that C&H would remain in operation were bolstered when the company agreed to relocate its corporate headquarters and 70 jobs to Crockett from Concord; C&H also promised to renovate a vacant park and refurbish a decrepit residence hotel on Loring Avenue; the developers pledged to hire as many locals as practical; Energy National, through its Pacific Generation parent, made a $250,000 contribution to the Crockett Improvement Association for local projects; and Pacific Generation will also fund a regional plan for recreational access to the local waterways, in coordination with the State Lands Commission.

Forging financial concessions was sometimes easy, and sometimes not. In one case, the developers and local schools could not agree on an impact fee related to additional students brought into the community by the development. The quandary was solved in a tangible way at the community celebration, as Pacific Generation president Brian Holt handed over a check for $65,000 to school officials to pay for a computer technology center at John Swett High School.

Some might say the economic benefits package offered by Crockett cogeneration developers is a form of sanctioned bribery. But the amount of money involved is really only a small fraction of the massive budget for construction and operation of the plant, and of the potential profits for C&H Sugar, Energy National, its partners and its numerous contractors—including Bechtel and General Electric.

Far more important to the community—especially many who vehemently opposed the plant when it first came to light—was the fact that John Miller was willing to sit down and talk about problems big or small, real or perceived.

But it didn't stop with talk, the real key was the commitment to crafting solutions that truly fit the community's needs.

[September 1992/November 1993]

Under the Volcano: Of Men, Demons and the Goddess Pele

IT IS A UNIQUE EXPERIENCE to look across the breakfast table and watch plumes of steam rising from the black surface of a volcano crater. Here at the Volcano House, set against the lip of the huge Kilauea Caldera on the Big Island of Hawaii, that pleasure is available for the price of a cup of Kona coffee.

I am one of the more than a million tourists who will pass through the Hawaii Volcanoes National Park during 1990. A large percentage of these visitors will be Japanese vacationers who are driven in busloads up to Volcano House for a brief stop on their seemingly never-ending tour of sightseeing, photo snapping and souvenir shopping. In deference to those who will stay overnight, the rooms here feature not only the ubiquitous Gideon Bible but also a volume of the teachings of the Buddha (in English).

A random glance through that book brought forth an applicable metaphor for my self-assigned task of reporting on the controversies surrounding exploitation of the geothermal resource that lies beneath Kilauea. I will ask the Buddha to forgive my attempt at paraphrase.

A man may look at a river and see the life-giving power of water that nourishes him and feeds the fish and plants that he harvests. But a demon who is consumed by fire in the belly and receives great pain from drinking the water will look at that same river and see only death and an enemy. It is therefore useless, says Buddha, to try to talk about this river to these two creatures, for they will never understand what you are trying to say.

Though I would never try to characterize which side represents man and which is demon, that same kind of disparity of understanding is at play regarding geothermal development now underway in the forest of Wao Kele o Puna, adjacent to the national park.

To the governor of Hawaii, the HECO utility, several private developers, Honolulu newspaper editors and many residents of the power-hungry islands of Oahu and Maui, geothermal is a potential alternative to imported oil addiction and a source of economic development that could lessen the dependence on sugarcane harvesting, macadamia nut processing and mai-tai serving for employment opportunities.

Oil provides 90 percent of the state's energy; that is a fact often repeated in the State Energy Resources report that articulates the need to diversify power sources. Andrea Beck, energy field representative for the Department of Business and Economic Development, told me that the only reason the islands survived the Arab oil-embargoes of the 1970s is that OPEC didn't realize that Hawaii is part of the USA until the very end. The state will probably not be so lucky if there is a next time.

To some Hawaiian natives and a small but highly vocal group of environmental defenders, geothermal development will destroy the Puna rainforest home of the ohi'a lehua tree (sacred to the volcano fire goddess Pele, I am told), and the few remaining species of indigenous birds. The surface of the land here is quite fragile; for at least one mile and a million geological years below it consists of layer upon layer of lava now barely covered with two inches of topsoil that has taken decades to form.

The ohi'a tree holds not just native religious significance; the forest is a seedbed for restoring life to the lands that are continually destroyed by volcanic flows, says Annie Szvetecz, Hawaiian project coordinator for the Rainforest Action Network.

Activists from the network, along with the local Pele Defense Fund and others, demonstrate regularly at the security gate that now bars access to a university-sponsored exploratory drilling site and—2.5 miles down the newly bulldozed road—the initial well pad and generation site for what could be a 500 MW inter-island power and transmission project developed by private interests on behalf of HECO. Another rally with music, mime and "the potential for non-violent civil disobedience" is set for March 24-25, according to the flyer I saw posted atop the drilling rig.

"Sunday brunch with the activists," is how geologist and drilling consultant John Deymonaz characterized the frequent protests that muster as many as 150 participants. Increasingly, these brunches feature arrests and the exchange of taunts as heated as the volcanic steam.

As is common in disputes that have gone on for years without resolve, things have reached a kind of development-at-any-cost versus righteous obstructionism dichotomy, and extreme voices can be heard.

I picked up a copy of a Maui-based periodical published by "the Obstreperous Patriot," which featured—among its libertarian-tinged articles on the Trilateral Commission plot to impose one-world government—an editorial depicting new energy source production as "unquestionably the signal for a further spate of building and tourist overdevelopment" that is linked to a plan to strip-mine manganese from the Pacific Ocean floor. The same paragraph of this full-page diatribe alludes to the "designs of the military," unspecified but presumably associated with the usurpation of the Bill of Rights.

These kinds of arguments do no good for those with legitimate concerns over the impacts of development. The tourist resorts will spread, whether the electricity is provided by the utility, by private entrepreneurs or by self-installed cogeneration machines bought from Sears.

I see from new Federal Energy Regulatory Commission filings there are plans for a 10 MW hydro plant on Hilo's Wailuko River and an 8 MW Chevron cogeneration plant for Ewa Beach, Hawaii; each project will encounter its own controversy over environmental impacts.

As for individual freedoms, well, the Patriot may say what he believes; I don't have to subscribe.

Less than fully convincing are the arguments I heard that the Puna forest does not really qualify as a rainforest under the "classic definition," or that it is unique to the world and will completely be destroyed, as some contend. I observed Puna to contain a beautiful and unusual forest in a rain belt (over 50 inches so far this year) that supports rare species and holds a special cultural place to devotees of ancient religions. Also apparent is that there are vast expanses of the same flora and the same birds singing throughout the Big Island, in the national park and on the Saddle Road between Mauna Loa and Mauna Kea volcanoes.

An article from the *Los Angeles Times* informs me that these species are threatened with extinction throughout the Hawaiian Island chain, not just from energy and land development, but from mongooses, snails and vines introduced over the past hundreds of years. Geothermal is obviously not the sole, or even major threat.

The defense of rainforests worldwide is a critical and necessary endeavor—in part because of the concern over ozone depletion and greenhouse effect—but it can be argued that geothermal displacement of oil-burning is more effective on an acre-for-acre basis than forest land preservation, at least for the job of promoting cleaner air.

I can understand the skepticism of those who do not trust any government entity to preserve—in a pristine condition—lands or cultural artifacts. On the western Hawaiian shore is the incongruous sight of ancient native petroglyphs carved in lava stone, surrounded by manicured golf courses and plaid-clad players on the private lands now occupied by the tribes of Sheraton, Westin and Hyatt.

The meaning of the dimpled orange ball-shaped artifact I discovered among the symbols will undoubtedly puzzle future archaeologists as much as the petroglyphs.

This is not an ideal example of preservation. But I know that change never ceases, even in lands intelligently purchased by the Nature Conservancy, and I will plead guilty of encouraging a moderate approach to energy development marked by intelligent exploitation and sane restrictions that balance competing needs.

The gulf separating positions on Hawaiian geothermal is, I am afraid, wider than the Kilauea Caldera. Adamant local opposition to geothermal development has extended to threaten a 25 MW project being pursued by Ormat Energy's Puna Geothermal Venture. This site is not in rainforest, but in a proven geothermal reserve on private land zoned for a papaya plantation. Its power will not be transported across mountain and undersea, but will be used on the Big Island to displace oil and to support direct-use possibilities that might realistically improve local economic options. And it promises a technology that some in the industry hail as "everything that geothermal should be" for its environmentally and economically beneficial design that returns steam to the earth for reuse with minimal sulfur emission.

I do not, however, favor the primacy of geothermal development over land protection or homeowner rights. There is, to my mind, a critical difference between an appropriately sized project that produces power where it is needed and a mega-sized 500 MW crapshoot dependent upon unproven steam resources and unprecedented underwater cable placement.

[March 1990]

All Steamed Up About Hawaiian Geothermal

THE KONA POWER BLACKOUT BEGAN EXACTLY AT 7:30 ON FRIDAY EVENING, about mid-way through our dinner of broiled mahi mahi and split pea soup at the Aloha Theater Cafe in Kainaliu. The food servers quickly brought individualized auxiliary lighting systems to the tables on the cafe's open porch, allowing us to navigate our meal by starlight and candles.

The power disruption caught us by surprise only because we had just arrived on the Big Island. In short order, we knew when to listen for the daily radio announcements of rolling outages planned by utility HELCO and where to check in the *West Hawaii Today* newspaper to see which sections of the island would be scheduled for a 45-minute blackout each evening. Forewarned, we picked up a supply of candles at the local variety store so future outages would seem less of an inconvenience and more of a vacation adventure. Had we stayed at one of the expensive resort hotels along the coast or in downtown Kona, though, we wouldn't have experienced any disruption because HELCO kept the energy flowing to these facilities to appease the more affluent tourists.

HELCO's rolling blackouts were necessitated by the temporary loss of two generating resources; the 10 MW Shipman No. 3 steam turbine had a thrust bearing failure one week before our arrival and when HELCO brought its 7.5 MW Hilo Combustion Turbine No. 1 out of standby to meet the load, the old turbine broke down under the strain. Both units are swiftly approaching the end of their useful lives; much like downtown Hilo, they are relics of the 1950s and are simply not up to meeting the demands of a fast-growing 1990's Hawaiian economy.

Development of new shopping malls on Hilo's outskirts, new residential subdivisions and coastal resort hotels throughout the island has outpaced the addition of new power generation and now brings the utility to the very edge of system reliability. In a letter to the editor of the *Honolulu Advertiser* last week, HELCO president Dan Williamson denied skimping on system maintenance but admitted, "We could spend five billion dollars over the next five years—five times our current capital budget—and still not be able to guarantee 'uninterrupted delivery of electricity' to our customers. Things go wrong."

Evening peak demand levels on the island reached 132 MW that week, severely cutting into reserve margins for the 135 MW capacity of the utility-owned system. HELCO also purchases 28 MW of power from independent producers, but that resource was largely unavailable. The 18 MW biomass plant at Hilo Coast Processing Company was off-line since April 5 for scheduled maintenance; the 10 MW Hamakua Sugar cogeneration unit unexpectedly dropped off-line temporarily as well.

In all, this was a tight situation for utility dispatchers that remained touch-and-go until Hilo Coast Processing accelerated its return to generation. The rescue did not come without cost; utility ratepayers will foot the bill for $100,000, according to emergency legislation approved by state legislators in Honolulu.

Ironically, throughout the power squeeze another potential resource could not be employed—not because of a technical problem but due to legal controversy. The 25 MW Puna Geothermal Venture, fully constructed and ready to generate, could not do so because of a stay imposed April 21 by Judge Kimura of the Third Circuit Court.

The stay, essentially an extension of a two-week temporary restraining order previously secured by opponents of geothermal development on the island, precludes until May 29 any activities at the site that might result in emitting hydrogen sulfide (H2S) into the atmosphere.

Even though the geothermal project features a closed-system design that is supposed to prevent H2S emissions, the owners of the plant, OESI (Ormat) of Nevada and the Constellation Energy subsidiary of Baltimore Gas & Electric, were taking a strict interpretation and would not begin operations until the date specified by the judge. The 25 MW geothermal project sat idle throughout the Big Island's rolling blackouts.

The legal stay is another in a long series of delays experienced by the Puna project. Originally contracted to begin power deliveries by October 1991, the developers hit a snag last June while drilling a production well; instead of finding the narrow, low pressure steam fissure they were seeking, the drillers apparently tapped into a crack in the earth more directly connected to the high pressure reservoir. The resulting uncontrolled release of vapor and H2S caused neighbors to evacuate their homes and further fueled the hot feelings against the project among local environmental activists and some residents of the nearby town of Pahoa. The well pad where the blowout took place has since been reconfigured from a production well to a reinjection well, and new restrictions added to the project's already stringent environmental permits. All told, the delays encountered at the site and in court pushed the Puna project's on-line date well past its contractual deadline, and the developers face much higher costs and an economic penalty of as much as $1 million.

The court stay, however, has little to do with this incident, according to Puna's project manager Steve Morris. Instead, the ruling was a response to a legal challenge of health permits issued to a larger and more speculative geothermal project planned in the Wao Kele o Puna rainforest, about 10 miles away. The permits issued to the proposed 500 MW Kilauea project and the Puna Geothermal Venture included maximum levels for sulfur emissions, even though the state's Department of Health had not formally conducted hearings to establish legal standards.

Opponents of geothermal, though small in number, are adept at using the legal process to incur delays and add to costs, suggested OESI's Steve Morris. Judge Kimura's stay does not directly challenge the Puna permits, but questions the rules that health officials used to issue the permits. Currently the department has a draft set of rules for H2S emissions under consideration, which OESI expects will be in place in time to begin commercial operations by June 1.

This recent trip only confirmed my initial feelings that the island activists have been blinded by their opposition to any geothermal development, no matter how it might contribute to the local economy or the necessary diversification of utility resources.

[May 1992]

It's My Backyard, Too

FROM THE BACK PORCH OF MY HOME, looking east to the San Francisco Bay, I can see the tips of smoke stacks at PG&E's Hunters Point generating station. The rest of the facility is blocked by the Thurgood Marshall Junior High School building. But I know it's there and can tell just by looking out the window when the plant is running and which way the wind is blowing.

In any event, I get a wide-angle shot of the Hunters Point/Bayview industrial panorama—including PG&E's Potrero station—each afternoon when I take Chelsea the dog for a walk to the top of Bernal Heights for the daily "doggy happy hour." This is a routine Chelsea and I have followed for more than six years, so she is well familiar with the scene and the scents.

Recently, something new appeared at the top of Anderson Street at Bernal Heights Boulevard. A large hand-made poster attached to a kitchen chair proclaimed a "Pollution Alert" and declared the intersection of Anderson and Bernal to be the point of greatest emission impacts from the proposed power plant. Other signs soon appeared to herald a community meeting about the plant, to be held this week at the Cortland Avenue community center.

Initially, I had a hard time believing that pollution from the Port would consistently find its way to the top of the hill. Virtually every day of our walks—no matter what time of day—the wind blows steadily, sometimes mightily, from the west. For four years, I even lived on Anderson Street, just a few houses below the top of the hill, and I recall the same easterly wind pattern. And yet, here was a flyer claiming that deadly pollutants from the project located two miles to the east would be raining down on Bernal 40 percent of the time.

BERNAL HEIGHTS GETS MAXIMUM EXPOSURE, WHY WEREN'T WE NOTIFIED?

The flyer contained other health and safety assertions that I found alarming: a purported 15 percent increased risk of deaths from particulate pollution, and the threat of a noxious ammonia cloud spewing from the plant. There were also bold statements that the plant is unfair to electric ratepayers, that it will provide "guaranteed profits" to SF Energy, and that this is all part of the deregulation plot to "subsidize cheap power for Big Users." There were also the now-familiar "environmental justice" arguments against Bayview hosting another toxic plant, and the query "Does San Francisco even need a third power plant?"

In short, I was confronted with an instance of the Not In My Backyard (NIMBY) syndrome. This time, it wasn't just any old backyard, it was my own backyard.

The scene at the neighborhood center was much like others I'd encountered literally hundreds of times in a 20-year career as a community reporter. A small room chock-full of neighbors. Familiar faces and some not so familiar chatting, hugging or just looking bored, waiting. A table filled with flyers, petitions and related activist sign-up sheets. A video camera and an intermittent sound system. All representatives of government and the dreaded developers readily identified by their suits and ties while everyone else dressed casually.

The agenda was packed by plant opponents; in fact, the developer's representative and a lone supporter were not granted their three minutes of speaking time until the very end of the night. I suppose that is the right of the organizers, but I found myself thinking that if the meeting was so obviously stacked to the other point of view, people might feel they were being railroaded.

I cannot, however, denigrate the opinions or worries of my neighbors, even if I judged them to be influenced by NIMBY fears and selective manipulation of information, as exemplified by the meeting flyers. For many, this was the first time they'd really thought about the impacts of the power plant, although it has been going through a regulatory siting process for more than a year, with numerous public hearings held less than a mile away—albeit "on the other side of the tracks" from Bernal. For others, especially those with small children and legitimate health concerns, the meeting provided a focal point for their apprehensions.

Dramatic emotions were on display: a breast cancer survivor who just knows her disease was caused by air pollution; an artist/mother/organizer who drew vivid verbal images of exploding gas pipelines and toxic ammonia clouds felling school children after the big earthquake; a compelling African-American neighborhood organizer, fluent in both the pulpit of public persuasion and the language of the streets—his message: you don't really need technical experts to know you don't want this plant staring you in the face, and you can't really trust the regulators because they are just as bad as the developers.

But those were the extremes. Personally, I found more cogent: the logic of a municipal energy analyst who traced the money flow out of the local economy and suggested that an equivalent amount spent on energy efficiency would be a better deal; a female neighbor who questioned the health standards and statistical yardsticks that are based on limited studies of men, not women; another woman who acknowledged the evident anti-project bias of the meeting but held it as an "antidote" to the formal hearings that, because of length and detail, exhaust continued public participation to the benefit of paid proponents of development.

I was persuaded that, indeed, the wind does blow from the east—though I'm not convinced it will do so 40 to 70 percent of the time that the plant is running, as one speaker claimed.

Towards the end of the meeting, I did something I hadn't done in many years. I shed my reporter's cloak of objectivity and got up to speak to my neighbors, explaining my interest in the issue. Unlike anyone else who spoke, I said, I had been following the plant since its inception and had still not decided to be in favor or against it. But I urged them to go beyond the "facts" and fears of the flyer, to read the public record compiled by the California Energy Commission and to contact CEC staff to answer their questions about the plant and how it has tried to mitigate every environmental complaint thrown at it. I even suggested the plant might make a positive contribution to the community, if forced to.

I still haven't made up my mind, and I continue to honor the arguments on both sides of the matter—and hope I've done no injustice to them in this account. But I can say this, based on many years of exposure to NIMBY issues: There will always be opponents to new development, some with very legitimate worries and fears that will linger for years.

Whether or not the CEC grants siting approval (I expect it will, though heavily conditioned for environmental concerns), the real question to be answered for SF Energy to successfully win over the community is not that of "need," or of reduced pollution, or of competitive advantage in a restructured industry. It is whether SF Energy has really made its case as a positive contributor to the city and to the affected neighborhoods. Despite pledges of jobs and local financial support, of promised "safe" operations—even in the face of the inevitable "Big One"—that is something the developers have not yet fully proven, as evidenced by the turnout at the Bernal Heights community center and similar sessions in Bayview.

[September 1995]

Obituary for a Power Plant

DEPENDING ON HOW YOU VIEW IT, Monday's action by the San Francisco Board of Supervisors was either a great victory for community environmental activism or a triumph of NIMBY fears over rational discourse.

Not that there was much chance of discourse at this stage of the game. When invited to introduce her resolution against construction of San Francisco Energy's proposed 240 MW cogeneration plant in the Bayview/Hunters Point neighborhood, supervisor Angela Alioto proclaimed a basic lesson of politics: "When you've got the votes, go for it. This can go out without even talking about it."

She almost regretted that a few moments later, when the first two supervisors polled voted NO against the resolution. "Wait!" Alioto screamed at her colleagues. "We're doing Hunters Point!"

The initial vote was rescinded and recast—resulting in a 10-to-zip approval with one member absent. Amos Brown, the newest supervisor and one of two who changed his vote, admitted, "I thought I voted against the plant."

Brown's statement was nearly drowned out by the cheers and applause from about a hundred citizen activists in the audience. They were easy to spot, wearing yellow "No Power Plant" badges and "Clean Up Bayview/Hunters Point" T-shirts, and waving "No Dirty Deals for Dirty Power" posters. The placards depicted projected toxic-emission statistics for the plant and decried the unbuilt project's potential effects on health in the neighborhood.

Before the session, the activists formed a lively picket line on the Van Ness Avenue sidewalk and then carried their street theater up into the board meeting room with them. "This is just like in the good old days, when the chambers were filled with people who cared," Alioto declared with pride.

The few supporters of the project sat quietly during the vote, then gathered up their materials and headed out the door. Except for one woman—obviously a disappointed member of the establishment coalition that favored the plant for its promised economic benefits (some of which went directly into their pockets, activists charged)—who stayed behind to heckle Alioto and seethe in anger. Eventually she left, too, and the board moved on to its exhausting trudge through the dozens of less-colorful action items and resolutions on the weekly agenda.

Left on the floor of the room was a carpet of sparkle and confetti, crumpled leaflets, discarded posters, and any chance that this particular power plant will ever be built.

Although developers of the cogeneration plant continue to express hope they can win approval, it is highly unlikely to happen. The problem is that they never quite understood how things work in San Francisco. And they seriously underestimated the neighborhood activists' antipathy for the project and the potency of the health-impact arguments against it.

While developers AES and SONAT managed to win regulatory approval and some supporters in the community, they never became part of the community—despite taking the name San Francisco Energy Company. SF Energy was easily targeted as an out-of-state, multinational corporation trying to make a profit off the deteriorating health of the local population. From the anti-plant materials and public testimony of opponents, one would think AES was like Nike, heartlessly pillaging third-world countries to bolster its bottom line.

Activists rallied against the company's early public relations embarrassments, its "astroturf" community organization, and the undisputed fact that Bayview/ Hunters Point needs help—but not another power plant.

The irony is that the proposed cogeneration plant is far better environmentally than the Pacific Gas & Electric projects that still operate in the area. And it was far cheaper than PG&E's plan to repower Hunters Point Unit 3. But proponents never convinced the activists that they will successfully displace those ancient units; indeed they never even convinced PG&E to sign a power purchase agreement.

They never capitalized on the anti-PG&E fervor of public power advocates, and they never figured out a way to direct their lower-cost energy right to the neighborhoods most affected by their operations.

Now, no matter what they do, it is too late.

As long as San Francisco Energy Company relied on the "rational discourse" of regulatory licensing proceedings or lease negotiations, it believed the project had a chance. Once the issue hit the emotional level of local politics, all chances went out the window.

[June 1996]

NIMBY by the Bay

RARELY DOES THE DEVELOPER OF A CONTROVERSIAL POWER PLANT get a second chance to win support from a community that is dead-set against allowing anything to be built in its backyard.

It happened once in Fresno, after GWF's 27 MW Hanford project switched from burning coal to a cleaner fuel mix and won back the good graces of local residents, regulators and the courts. People even forgave the mayor and the project's manager for having an affair during the permitting process. It happened again in Crockett after a new owner began the regulatory process from scratch and effectively wooed the skeptical townsfolk into accepting a 240 MW cogen plant as a community asset rather than a NIMBY liability.

Perhaps most miraculously of all, it happened in Hunters Point. Against all odds, the San Francisco Energy Company successfully changed its image from that of an outsider and a perpetrator of "environmental racism" into that of a community-based business, restoring economic vitality to a blighted neighborhood and eventually helping San Francisco to municipalize its electric utility services.

All SF Energy had to do was cede part ownership of the 240 MW project to a neighborhood economic development agency. That—plus hiring Willie Mays as president of the local company and bankrolling Angela Alioto's successful race for the mayor's seat—was all it took. San Francisco may have lost PG&E in the process, but it regained its stature as "The City That Knows How."

They say it's always darkest just before dawn. Indeed, prospects looked pretty bleak for the cogeneration plant by late 1995. A product of the ill-fated resource auction mandated by the California Public Utilities Commission, the SF cogen plant faced trouble from the start.

After federal regulators declared the auction process illegal and the CPUC suspended all resulting contracts, SF Energy's owners tried to argue their plant was not implicated in the violation. "We signed our contract before the FERC decision, which specifically stated that existing contracts are not affected by the new all-source bidding rule," explained Bob Greenfield, development executive for the owners. "Besides," he added, "PG&E was not a party to that case. FERC only said that Edison and SDG&E could not be forced to sign contracts."

The CPUC did not agree. Regulators were so flustered by the FERC ruling they imposed yet another a stay on all the contracts until they devised a solution that, unfortunately, left SF Energy in limbo. CPUC president William Daniel Lawyer reasoned that since FERC required an all-source bid to determine utility avoided-costs, the utilities would have to redo the auction—this time allowing all comers into the competition. But time was limited. The first auction took years to design and conduct, and independent power bidders made it clear they would boycott any new, lengthy process.

The solution, Lawyer decided, was to graft a small "integrated bidding pilot" being conducted by PG&E into the new solicitation. The 50-200 MW size of the auction was expanded to 6000 MW, incorporating the previous solicitation and two new "identified deferrable resource" benchmarks: PG&E's Diablo Canyon nuclear plant and Edison's two remaining SONGS nuclear units. Lawyer's plan killed several birds with a single stone: it took care of the all-source bidding requirement; it opened the utilities' nuclear assets to competition instead of allowing the expensive special rate settlements proposed by DRA and the IOUs; and it saved ratepayers billions of dollars in stranded nuclear costs. Once the nuclear plants were beaten by the competition, they were cut out of rate-base and became the sole liability of the utility shareholders.

But the plan excluded SF Energy because PG&E was able to argue that any resources located on the San Francisco peninsula could not displace utility resources on constrained transmission lines in and out of the city. Just as the project benefited from limited competition in the first bid process because of transmission constraints; it was cut out of the new competition for the same reason.

Things got worse. The California Energy Commission decided that since the auction was now illegal, it could no longer automatically determine that winning resources were "needed" under the state's resource plan. Local opponents of the SF cogen plant seized the opportunity presented by Fate and pursued an all-out attack on the proposed project.

At every public forum on the project—whether held by the CEC, the Port of SF, the Board of Supervisors, local permitting agencies, or even on public access cable TV—the NIMBY activists turned out in full force. They argued against the legality of siting the plant. They contested the determination of need. They pressed their claims of economic piracy and environmental racism against the developers.

They portrayed SF Energy's executives as out-of-town raiders who cared only about their own profits without regard for the community's well-being. Local newspapers, especially neighborhood papers like the SF *Bay Anarchist*, The Independence and The Meekly, took to calling the developer "SF Enemy." Editors of the mainstream press, the *Chronic-Ill* and the *SF Exhausted*, sided with PG&E and opposed the plant.

Stung by the criticism and mounting legal costs, one of the project's development partners—a gas pipeline company—pulled out. Bob Greenfield, the sole remaining executive on the SF Energy team, faced a quandary. Should he give up the project as a failure, or should he fight for what he believed in?

It Happened in Hunters Point

Bob Greenfield was depressed. As he drained his drink, he briefly considered ordering another—but didn't. It wouldn't change anything. It wouldn't make his problems go away and it sure wouldn't help get this cogeneration plant built.

The day was a disaster and Bob couldn't help but feel he'd reached the end of his road. That morning, he received three fatal blows: the California Energy Commission's siting committee recommended against the San Francisco Energy Company's project, the Board of Supervisors rejected a revised lease agreement between the project and the Port, and a federal district court upheld FERC's determination that the BRPU auction was against the law. The $175 million power plant was sinking fast, without a bucket to bail it out.

Normally, Bob didn't drink. But here he was, sitting at the bar on a Thursday night watching the Six O'clock Bad News. Hunters Point and Bayview residents who opposed his cogeneration plant were celebrating for the cameras. "NIMBY by the Bay," was what the reporter called it. In a corner of the bar, PG&E workers from the nearby Hunters Point plant also celebrated, toasting champagne in beer mugs.

As he left Bo's Bountiful Bar and got into his car parked at the end of Cargo Way, Bob looked up at the back side of PG&E's Hunters Point station. He thought about all the work that went into planning this development to displace one of those utility units with private power. And about all the money he'd spent trying to convince residents that the project was a good one. The wasted effort was like acid smoke rising from the power plant's stacks.

He had high hopes after SF Energy "won" the BRPU auction—but then things went so completely awry. Of all the unfair accusations made against the plant, Bob was stung personally by the epithet "environmental racist" hurled by the community. "They just don't understand," he thought. "I guess they never will."

Preoccupied and disoriented by the dense fog, he didn't notice missing the right turn at 3rd Street until he reached a dead-end road overlooking Islais Creek Channel. "Arthur Street. Hmm, I never noticed it before," he thought. He got out of the car and walked down to the water's edge. Not much to see—rotting piers, half-submerged shopping carts and other debris. To the east he saw the dark outline of the 3rd St. drawbridge. A newspaper headline flashed in his mind—"Failed Power Plant Developer Leaps to Death from Levon Hagop Nishkian Bridge." Maybe it was fitting; the Golden Gate had never opened its arms wide to him. This sad little bridge with an implausible name might provide a proper end for his career.

The air smelled of the sea. What was it? Like crabs in boiling water. For a second, he felt nauseous.

"Don't you love that wonderful aroma?" a woman's voice came from the fog. Bob looked up startled, then he recognized her; it was Angela Alioto, the only county supervisor who voted in favor of his power plant. "Angela, where did you come from? And what is that awful perfume you're wearing?"

"Wrong. I'm Angela's Higher Power," she said. "Usually we're a package deal, but tonight she wanted to eat in North Beach again and I felt like going to the Old Clam House on Bayshore for some crab. I got a doggy bag. You hungry? Want some sourdough bread?"

"No thanks," he replied, forgetting for the moment his imagined suicide. "Thank Angela for me. Tell her goodbye. I guess I'll head back to Virginia tomorrow."

"Are you just giving up? I can't believe it. Let's take a walk over here." She tugged on his arm and led him into a small but well-tended garden at the end of Arthur Street. "Watch your step," she told him. Bob noticed the sign for the first time: Please Be Careful—Volunteer Restoration Project.

"What do you think San Francisco would be if people just gave up?" she suddenly berated him. "We'd still be a pile of rubble left after the 1906 earthquake, that's what. BankAmerica would still be a one-branch loan office at Fisherman's Wharf. The 49ers and the Giants would be sitting in the cellar instead of World Champions. The Presidio golf course would still be run by the Army. Angela and I would never get to be mayor. You can't just give up." She looked right into his soul. "It's just like this garden. This was a pile of garbage, junk and weeds. But San Franciscans took an interest and fixed it up. That's what I'm talking about."

"But we tried!" Bob protested. "We offered them jobs, and job training. We promised $50,000 to the neighborhood redevelopment agency. We flew people down to see our other operations in Los Angeles to prove we could be part of the community. They just called us racists and took our money anyway," he sulked. "And they hijacked the plane to Disneyland." The memory of the scandal still hurt.

"You gave. You offered. You promised. What is that? Listen to me. Those things are just handouts. There's no respect for the people involved. The only way you can save your power plant is by making it part of the community. You've got to give the people some juice. That's how things work here. And I'm not talking about a couple of lousy security guard jobs. You have to let these people own at least 40 percent of the plant."

"WHAT!" he cried.

"You heard me, 40 percent. And you have to hire executives from the community to run the partnership," she replied.

"My boss will never go for that. Who can we hire locally that's qualified to run this plant? You may not realize it but affirmative action doesn't work," Bob said in desperation.

"This is not affirmative action," Angela retorted. "This is how you can save your plant. You want to know who can make this work? Meet me at Candlestick Park tomorrow night. Section 112, Row 13, Seat 6A. You shouldn't have trouble getting a ticket."

With that, the Angel disappeared, leaving Bob completely bewildered.

The Angel From Left Field

Bob Greenfield turned away from the Candlestick Park ticket window empty-handed. He was here to meet Angela Alioto—or the being that claimed to be Angela's Higher Power—but he couldn't get into the park because the game was sold out. "The only game all season where more than 5,000 people even bought tickets," he thought.

The sell-out crowd wasn't because of the popularity of the current SF Giants. Like all other Major League teams that year, the Giants were made up of strike scabs, teen-aged wanna-be players and minor league washouts. True, it was August and they were still in contention for the division pennant—two games above .500 and one game out of 1st place—but only because the other teams were worse. Imagine an entire league rivaling the 1962 New York Mets for incompetence.

No, the reason for the sell-out was that it was "Old Timers' Night" featuring players from the glory years of baseball—star athletes whose names and faces people knew as well as their own. And 60,000 fans of the way things used to be were on hand for the festivities.

As Bob walked through the parking lot, a disheveled person approached. "Need a ticket? $50," he said, holding out a stub for Bob to examine. Section 112, Row 13, Seat 6A—exactly where Angela had told him to sit. Bob looked over his shoulder to make sure it wasn't a set-up by the scalper police, then gladly handed over a bill, took the ticket and rushed through the gate.

He didn't appreciate the full coincidence until he got to the box and sat down—an empty chair beside him. Third-base side, lower deck. It was exactly the same seat where, some 30 years before, Bob and his Dad saw a doubleheader while on vacation in San Francisco. And there, on the field, were many of the same players he rooted for as a child. A tinge of regret haunted him. How he had loved baseball players—whether they were black, white, Cuban, third-generation Irish, or whatever. That's why the charges of racism hurled by community opponents of the SF Cogeneration project hurt him so. He wasn't a racist—he never was.

"Great night for a game." Her voice snapped Bob out of his reverie. She was wearing a Giants cap and an orange softball shirt with the letters A.A.H.P. splayed across the front. "These Italian sausage sandwiches are great! Want some?"

"No, thanks," he said politely. "Angela, or whoever you are, this isn't going to work. I'll never get our investors to hand over 40 percent of the project to a bunch of community activists…"

"OK, 33 percent," she bargained, "But no less. Besides, what are your other options? To hang up your glove and head for the showers? You think that's what Juan Marichal did after he injured his arm in 1966? No. He came back and won 20 games."

"But Angela, nobody in San Francisco wants this power plant. No matter how we tried, we couldn't get people—real people—to come out in support."

"Look at all these people here tonight," she said gently. "Nobody has been to a game all season, so why are they here? To watch a bunch of bozos boot the ball across the field? No. They came because of players they respect and admire. And they'll come to you, and your plant, if you offer them the same thing."

"I don't get you," he said, looking down at the field.

Just then, the announcer began introducing some of the sports legends who were to play that night. "Bob, you asked who could make this work. There's your answer." She pointed to the Jumbotron screen above center field as ex-Giants Willie Mays and Willie McCovey were introduced. A riotous cheer rose from the stands.

"Mays & McCovey are the executives you need to hire," she said. "Two successful and trusted businessmen—African-American businessmen—who never left San Francisco. Put them in charge of your power plant and you'll get support from the neighborhood and respect from the politicians. Profits from the plant can be used to held clean up the neighborhood. Nobody will call you a racist. They'll call you a hero. But you gotta change the name of the company. SF Energy just doesn't cut it in the 'hood. I think 'The 24-44 Partnership' would be more appealing," she said, referring to the uniform numbers of the two players. "You gotta talk their talk."

"But Angela," Bob whined. "The project is dead. The resource auction is illegal. PG&E says it doesn't want or need the power. I don't even have a valid sales contract anymore."

"We can get you one with the city. When Angela and I become mayor, we are going to municipalize our utility service away from PG&E. We have Hetch Hetchy, but we need other solid resources. Your plant—and maybe another you can build in a couple of years—will give us about half of the power we need. We can buy the rest wholesale. But we need your plant! Together, we can get the whole city behind this."

Angela's political agenda began to show—municipalization was the keystone of her campaign. Bob didn't know what to think. Then she told him.

"Of course, Angela needs more than your project. She needs your support in the form of campaign contributions, as much as your company can give under the law. And from your contractors and consultants. You give, you get. That's politics. Yeah, I know. It's a dirty and despicable thing to ask for money. That's why I do it instead of Angela." As she had the night before, the spirit looked deeply into Bob, as if touching his psyche. "I'm serious. Do you need an omen? Like this is 'Field of Dreams' or something?"

As if on cue, the Jumbotron flashed a message that caught Bob's eye. It was the daily San Francisco Trivia Contest, but Bob felt it was aimed directly at him. "If you can answer this question, it proves you are a true San Franciscan at heart and this plan will work," Angela told him.

The question: Who are San Francisco's three drawbridges named after? Bob thought a moment. He drove over all three every night on his way home from the development sites in Hunters Point. The Francis 'Lefty' O'Doul bridge on 3rd St. Everyone knows that; Lefty was a former Giants player. The Peter Maloney bridge over 4th St. That's two. Bob racked his brain. Then it hit him—the Levon Hagop Nishkian bridge at Islais Creek. The very bridge he'd considered jumping from last night when he was in deep despair.

Bob turned to Angela, but she was nowhere to be seen. Somehow, deep in his heart, he knew everything was going to work out.

[March 1995]

Rich or Poor, Some Communities Will Not Roll Over

IT'S NOT UNUSUAL TO FIND A TENT ENCAMPMENT in front of a public building, occupied by citizens protesting some government act or unwanted commercial development in their community.

But it is highly unusual when the protestors include the mayor and vice mayor of the town.

Raul Moriel, mayor of South Gate, an economically distressed city in Los Angeles County, along with vice mayor Xochilt Ruvacaba, last week joined in a hunger strike and tent occupation on the street in front of their own city hall to protest possible construction of a new 550 MW power plant in South Gate by Sunlaw Energy.

Though the proposed Nueva Azalea facility boasted advanced air-quality controls, called Sconox, that the company claims to be the cleanest system available, the community opposed the project because it does not want any additional pollutants. The issue went beyond simple environmentalism, however, becoming one of "environmental justice" as the largely Latino community believes it is being unfairly burdened with a development meant to provide power for other parts of the state and profits for a company based elsewhere.

Mayor Moriel did not last very long in his hunger strike and had to be taken to the hospital after four days. But he made his point. On Tuesday, citizens of South Gate approved an advisory referendum against the development, and developer Sunlaw immediately asked for suspension of its certification process at the California Energy Commission.

Wayne Gould, president of Sunlaw, stressed a continued belief that the Sconox system to be employed at Nueva Azalea offered "unprecedented low NOx emissions" and that the facility would provide the kind of "safer, cleaner and more reliable" generation demanded by California's energy crisis. However, Gould said, "We've looked at our business plan and objectives and we've determined not to move forward with Nueva Azalea."

Not far away on a map—but a world apart in terms of demographics—the city of Huntington Beach is also in the midst of an antidevelopment fight. In this case, it is not a new facility but the proposed modernization and expansion of the Huntington Beach generating station. AES Corporation bought the Huntington Beach plant from Southern California Edison and has applied to the CEC for approval of a plan to upgrade units 3 and 4 of the aged facility, increasing available capacity and modernizing emissions controls to allow for increased operations.

Originally filed under the traditional CEC review process, the Huntington Beach project has become a pioneer of new expedited siting rules brought about by Governor Gray Davis' emergency declaration. Though the community had expressed its misgivings about the project meeting all of its concerns to begin with, the CEC siting committee this past week approved a 60-day review process for the upgrade project.

In the order, commissioners Art Rosenfeld and Bob Pernell acknowledged the bind. "The commission's traditional, 12-month AFC process cannot meet the governor's goal of bringing significant new generating capacity online for summer of 2001." AES could complete the upgrade in 90 days, the CEC noted. "Based on simple arithmetic, 90 days of construction subtracted from the beginning of 2001 summer peak loads requires certification of the retooling project in early to mid-April 2001."

Though bowing to "the objectives of environmental protection and protection of public health and safety," the CEC committee adopted an expedited schedule for the project.

During a recent public hearing on the project, CEC project manager Jack Caswell admitted the difficulties faced by the siting staff. "It's going to be a tough, tough process here. I have great concerns about how to get this done," he said.

The complexity of the case was underscored when the city submitted to the CEC a 27-page list of the environmental and economic conditions it wants to have imposed on the AES project. Air quality, ocean quality and visual impacts top the city's list, but there were also demands for a $1-million community contribution plus requirements that 20 percent of the work force be hired locally and 25 percent of procurement come from local vendors.

The city wants the company to build an effluent pipe more than one mile long to limit beach pollution, but most importantly, it wants to be put in charge of monitoring the construction program, with powers to halt or further condition operations if AES violates any part of the package.

And that was just part one of Huntington Beach's list. The city's hired attorney promised further details after CEC staff issue their assessment.

"We're not trying to stop the power plant," attorney Al Pak told me this week. "We want to make sure that if it's operating, it's a good neighbor. We want to see all the impacts mitigated."

But the city also wants a novel condition attached—that all power from the upgraded facility be sold within California, with similar limits on AES' operations at Los Alamitos and Redondo Beach to prevent those plants from being pressed into the service of unfettered interstate commerce. "We want to put handcuffs on the other plants," Pak said, stating that this, of course, would be a "voluntary" agreement by the developer.

These two cases, representing a minority community willing to go to political and physical extremes to prevent any generation development, and an affluent community pushing the envelope of legal argument to make sure its concerns are met, may be taken as harbingers of the coming battles over the siting of power plants in California.

There are other prominent examples, such as the Metcalf plant in San Jose, which has been getting plenty of media attention. Conversely, there are a few instances where communities, such as the cities of Hayward and Escondido, either have shown great willingness to host a new power facility or are actively recruiting such development.

California regulators have a daunting task ahead of them to compress a lengthy and detailed public review of projects into a matter of weeks. Prospective developers are cast in a dual role, as saviors of a faltering energy system and as suspected plunderers of public resources. Community activists face an uphill struggle made even more difficult by the crisis mentality and the rush to fill holes in a deteriorating energy infrastructure.

But it should be obvious, at least from the two examples given above, that opponents of development are not going to simply roll over, despite emergency declarations by politicians.

[March 2001]

Between Regulation and Reality
Lies Playa del Rey

WHEN THE CASE BEGAN, it appeared to be little more than a routine transaction. Southern California Gas in May 1999 had asked the California Public Utilities Commission to approve its pending sale of some properties located along the periphery of its Playa del Rey gas storage fields, northwest of the Los Angeles International Airport and a few miles south of Marina del Rey.

The land was no longer needed for storage operations, and the existing wells had been capped and abandoned, SoCal Gas said in its filing. The matter was so routine that the utility claimed CPUC approval was not even necessary, and it cited lot sales in the area over the previous 50 years that had been completed without regulatory review. Because commission rules about how net sales proceeds should be split between utility shareholders and ratepayers had changed, SoCal Gas wanted to make sure its dealings were on the record. The $17 million price for the lots was more than ten times their book value, and SoCal Gas proposed a 50/50 split of the $9 million after-tax gains. Ratepayers would get a $4.6 million rate reduction out of the deal.

On the surface, a noncontroversial matter that could be wrapped up within four months, SoCal Gas said, and it asked the commission for an expedited process "so that buyers of the property may improve these lots at the earliest time possible and the benefits of the sale can be realized…at the earliest possible date." The contracts were already signed, but the gas company said it would not transfer title until the CPUC signed off on the sales.

Normally, such an application would pass unnoticed, and particularly during a time when the entire structure of utility regulation was undergoing a seismic shift. Regulators were preoccupied with the multitude of issues surrounding electric restructuring, and even those who paid closest attention to natural gas matters were embroiled in a proceeding meant to inject more competition into company operations while at the same time trying to deal with the impacts that electricity deregulation was having on pipeline system capacity rights and costs.

As the case entered its preliminary stages, the issues were predictable. Rate-payer advocates argued with the utility over the allocation of proceeds. The Office of Ratepayer Advocates questioned the tax treatment proposed by SoCal Gas, and The Utility Reform Network said that ratepayers should get 90 percent of the gains, not just half. However, neither group objected to the sale itself.

So it was something of a surprise when a couple of local environmental activists started kicking up a fuss at the CPUC regarding the proposed lot sales. Calling themselves the Grassroots Coalition/Friends of the Animals and Ballona Wetlands Forever/Spirit of the Sage Council, the two women who petitioned for late intervention in the case appeared to be bringing a host of unrelated concerns and complaints into what was by all indications a straightforward transaction.

Kathy Knight of Ballona Wetlands and Patricia McPherson of the Grassroots Coalition saw the sale of lots not only as one more incursion of development into the rare open spaces along the coast but as a potential health hazard to anyone who might build homes or businesses on the lots sitting on top of a major natural gas storage field.

They wanted the CPUC to investigate whether it made any sense to allow the sales, and further, they hoped for a deeper investigation of the utility's storage operations.

The important issue was not how to split the sales proceeds, they claimed, but that the entire area was "inherently unsafe" because of leaking toxic gases. Not just the lots at Playa del Rey, but an entire geologic zone that stretched up to toney Marina del Rey and encompassed existing homes and a planned new development called Playa Vista being promoted by well-regarded developers with full endorsement and financial participation of the city and county of Los Angeles.

"SoCal Gas has an underground reservoir," McPherson explained. "They're injecting billions of cubic feet of gas into the ground. That affects the Playa Vista Bluff, Marina del Rey and Ballona Wetlands. There are over 300 underground storage fields in the US. This is the only city that's attempting to build right over one."

She cited a parallel case involving SoCal's Montebello storage fields, where she said leaks forced the utility to tear down homes and even the city hall in order to find and mitigate problems. When the utility had tried to sell off Montebello properties, it failed to disclose the environmental risks and misled regulators, she alleged. "We need to address the issue that all of these wells are going to leak," she said. If you build a house on a problem area, how are you going to bring in equipment necessary to explore for leaks and fix the problem?

For Knight, the situation posed severe health risks in an area that she and McPherson had been investigating for years. "We've been finding people who don't even know their home is over a well. They're sick, their children are sick." Knight pointed to a long-running personal injury lawsuit filed by Lyn Stadish against the utility.

Stadish claimed that she contracted cancer from exposure to benzene and other gases released from the storage fields. Though the company was fighting the allegations with all its legal might, the simple fact of Stadish's illness was more than enough proof of a severe health risk in the area, Knight alleged. "If the CPUC said OK to this, the CPUC could be liable for problems in the future."

The utility resisted the activists' involvement in the case and their requests for a full environmental review of the properties. "Not only are the allegations of the Ballona Group irrelevant to this proceeding, they are patently false," the utility told the commission. The claim that the entire area was unsafe because of gas leaks "has been repeatedly rejected by those local agencies with jurisdiction over the construction of buildings in this area generally and the development of the Ballona Wetlands area in particular."

While special protections are needed for construction over old wells, SoCal countered that "There are thousands of abandoned oil and gas wells in the Los Angeles basin, and buildings are safely constructed over or adjacent to such wells all of the time." Besides, the utility continued, environmental review and safety mitigation "are items of local concern, not matters raised for this commission by this application." When SoCal offered a preliminary environmental assessment in June 2000, it continued to deny that its wells or storage facility had ever been shown to leak.

Of course, the activists were not dissuaded, but the surprise was that they began chipping away at the commission's resistance to widening the scope of the case to include environmental considerations and a more intense assessment of the properties in question. Assigned judge Carol Brown even arranged for a staff tour of the properties last year.

In addition, McPherson's Grassroots Coalition has helped coordinate three individual complaints against SoCal Gas, alleging leaks at the facilities. The cases are not consolidated with the lot sale application, but both are being handled by ALJ Brown, who has hinged the complaints proceeding on the environmental work done for that case. Brown also recently ordered a health assessment that the utility had been resisting.

What made the difference in overcoming regulatory indifference? Persistence and evidence, said McPherson. "It's been very difficult, but the more information we've garnered, the more we've been vindicated. There's a lot of not fessing up to the truth, and we have the data to prove otherwise."

The activists have had problems conforming to the nuts and bolts of regulatory filings and made some missteps that brought objections from the utility and an admonition from the judge.

"That's the trouble with citizens," Knight admitted. "You're doing this for the first time in your lives and you make mistakes. I'm volunteering 60 hours a week to this. I can't become an expert in how to file something at the CPUC."

Both of the women praised the commission staff for assistance in figuring out the complexities of procedure and were especially grateful to ALJ Brown for being willing to listen and respond to what they see as broader societal issues. Neither had anticipated getting much help from the CPUC at first, but they have come to see the agency's statutory mandate to protect the public health and safety with regard to utility operations as a wedge to help them achieve their goal of uncovering the truth about Playa del Rey, despite what they consider resistance by the utility, the city of Los Angeles and almost every other bureaucracy they have dealt with over the past decade. The CPUC is just one forum out of several they are pursuing.

McPherson said public agencies must take their responsibilities seriously. "We're dealing with companies that have not shared highly critical information that people need for health and safety." She raised issues of legal liability but emphasized that finding out what is really going on is still the top priority. If there are serious consequences regarding the development plans for Playa Vista and vicinity, that is an issue for the future.

"The most difficult thing we were encountering is getting real information," she concluded. "Once we have that information, it will lead the way. Disclosure is everything."

[September 2001]

0-595-33792-9

CPSIA information can be obtained at www.ICGtesting.com
Printed in the USA
LVOW06s2134220915

455344LV00001B/138/P